Everything You Need to Know about Estate

Everything You Need to Know about Estate Planning

Kevin Wark

KEY PORTER BOOKS

CANADIAN CATALOGUING IN PUBLICATION DATA

Wark, Kevin
    Everything you need to know about estate planning

ISBN 1-55263-346-2

1. Estate Planning – Canada – Popular works. I. Title.

KE5974.Z82W37 2001   346.7105'2   C00-933333-9
KF750.W37 2001

THE CANADA COUNCIL | LE CONSEIL DES ARTS
FOR THE ARTS | DU CANADA
SINCE 1957 | DEPUIS 1957

The publisher gratefully acknowledges the support of The Canada Council for the Arts and the
Ontario Arts Council for its publishing program.

We acknowledge the financial support of the Government of Canada through the Book Publishing
Industry Development Program (BPIDP) for our publishing activities.

Key Porter Books Limited
70 The Esplanade
Toronto, Ontario
Canada M5E 1R2
www.keyporter.com

Design: Peter Maher
Electronic formatting: Kim Monteforte, Heidy Lawrance Associates

Printed and bound in Canada

01 02 03 04 05 6 5 4 3 2 1

Acknowledgements

This book has its origins in an earlier publication that was technical in nature and designed for estate planners. I am thankful to Anna Porter for her initiative and support in converting the contents of that original publication into an estate planning guide for the general public. I also want to recognize the assistance of Gary Tannyan, who transformed fairly complex and dry concepts into an entertaining and meaningful publication. I am grateful to the many people at Equinox Financial Group who provided both moral and editorial support in the development of material. And finally, to my wife Sandy—thank you for your patience while I spent many evenings and weekends researching, writing, and proofing the final publication.

Contents

Introduction
Or, what's in it for you?

O ne thing is for sure: there are a lot of hands-on, do-it-yourself pioneers in this world. You know the type. The person who would rather lie on a cold, hard garage floor, get covered in grease, and repair a leaky oil pump than take the car to a mechanic. The person who doesn't trust financial experts and, equipped with a home computer, proceeds to precariously manage (or more likely mismanage) his or her personal finance portfolio over the Web. The person who, with the right how-to book, would try and take out their own appendix.

If you happen to be one of these spirited individuals, there's a good chance that this book is not for you. This book will not teach you how to become an estate planner. And it won't teach you how to create your own personalized estate plan. It's not meant to.

This book is for the rest of us. Those who are a little apprehensive and uncomfortable giving any thought at all to our own mortality. Those who figure it will all work out well enough in the end (denial is such an endearing human characteristic).

And let's not forget those who suffer involuntary deafness and glazing of the eyes at the mere mention of taxes, Registered Retirement Savings Plans (RRSPs), wills, insurance, and other issues, which might include legal jargon. This group must also include those souls who have not yet learned to program their VCRs.

Yes, this book is for you. You don't want to be an expert in the field. You would, however, appreciate a reasonable explanation (in plain English) of what's involved in estate planning, and how the various planning components may affect you and the ones you love.

For many Canadians, a discussion of getting one's affairs in order—or any contemplation of death, for that matter—is a morbid topic to be quickly shelved. But keep reading. Although death is the inescapable reason for organizing your estate, it is not always the overriding factor. How you plan your estate can have a positive impact on the way you *live*.

This book will make the subject of estate planning less mysterious, less confusing, and certainly less intimidating. I hope that, after reading the various chapters, you'll come away with the knowledge, enthusiasm, and confidence to work comfortably with a professional estate planner. That way, you and your family's best interests will be looked after properly, and nothing will be left to chance.

There will always be people who want to do everything on their own. Good for them. But for those of us (myself included!) who recognize that we can't do it all, the smart money is on getting expert help. I hope this book will inspire action in this often ignored aspect of our lives.

Here's what will be covered:

THE ESSENTIALS OF A SIMPLE ESTATE PLAN
- A current will
- Powers of attorney
- Life insurance for dependents and estate liabilities

STRATEGIES FOR LARGER AND MORE SOPHISTICATED ESTATES
- Tax reduction strategies while alive and upon death
- Charitable gifting programs
- Trust planning
- Health care directives
- Business succession programs
- Special programs for dependent beneficiaries
- Comprehensive investment and retirement programs
- Special insurance coverage for critical illness and long-term care

1
That's life!
Or, what else could happen next?

WHEN YOU GOT NOTHING,
YOU GOT NOTHING TO LOSE.
—Bob Dylan

B ad grammar aside, Bob Dylan makes a valid point. However, very few of us truly have nothing. Most of us have homes, RRSPs, bank accounts, mutual funds, and other material possessions. Most of us also have family, friends, pets, and favoured causes. While all of this usually brings a certain level of contentment, it also comes with a price—responsibility. In other words, if you have something, you definitely have something to lose.

That's life—full of challenges, disappointments, and troubles. A constant battle to "make the most of it." Planning for your death is just one more thing you need to deal with.

I don't know who the particular complainer was, but he or she made a fair assessment by observing that "dying is easy—life is hard." A proper estate plan won't take the sting out of dying, but it can make that hard life a little easier—both for you now, and for your family when your time to depart does arrive.

You don't have to be wealthy

Many people mistakenly believe that in order to have an estate plan in place, or a will made out, a fair degree of wealth should be involved. But regardless of whether you have assets that total hundreds of thousands of dollars, or more modest means, you should have an estate plan.

Even a young married couple with few financial assets should at least have wills and mutual powers of attorney in place (more details on these two items later).

Although many of us have experienced the premature loss of a family member or friend, most Canadians can expect to live to a ripe old age. In fact, the odds of living past 80 are constantly improving thanks to advances in modern medicine and our own increasing interest in more active lifestyles.

Canadians are living longer

Despite all the hand-wringing over the state of our health care system, Canadians are living longer, healthier lives than ever before. So the prospects are good that most of us will reach our late seventies or eighties, or even beyond. This happy piece of news makes it especially important to have strategies for dealing with longer life—the longer you live the more assets you can accumulate and the more money you will need to finance your retirement.

A regularly adjusted financial plan, together with a thoroughly thought-out estate plan, can free you from worrying about the future and preserve your current assets. It will allow your assets to grow and ensure that a large portion of what you don't spend during your lifetime will go to the ones you love.

We all recognize that life doesn't always go according to plan. In fact, it rarely does. That's why we have insurance on our homes, cars, and other valuables. You may never have occasion to use it, but you sleep better knowing it's there. An estate plan is no different. It provides a great level of comfort as you head towards the time in your life when you might need help blowing out all those candles on your birthday cake.

But an estate plan can really make a difference in the unlikely event of your premature demise. It will protect your survivors from all sorts of administrative and cash flow nightmares. It's nice to know things will be taken care of should the unmentionable happen.

Simple enough, right? Makes complete sense? Yet most Canadians are inadequately prepared for either eventuality—living a long prosperous life or leaving this planet a little early.

When trouble comes a-calling

The consequences of being unprepared can be devastating to surviving family members and business associates, compounding their grief with all sorts of troubles.

We've all heard stories of someone dying (prematurely or of old age) without a will. A whole heap of problems can crop up—think about funeral arrangements and disposition of assets, including family heirlooms, to name just two. It's one of the all-time guaranteed ways to kick-start a family feud—and it costs money at a time when a family can least afford extra expenses.

Aside from the wills, the other big issue that confronts a majority of Canadian families is the lack of life insurance or other liquid assets to cover cash requirements upon death. Financial planners from Corner Brook to Victoria know that most of us do not realize the *cost* of losing a spouse, grief aside.

If the major wage earner passes on, the existing insurance is often unable to make up the shortfall in income. Should the prime caregiver be the deceased, the cost of caring for the children and tending to the home become huge expenses. Sometimes, the surviving spouse has to leave his or her job to be home with the children. If the insurance doesn't provide for that type of lifestyle, it's likely that the family home will no longer be affordable, removing another stable aspect of life from the picture.

Don't be fooled into thinking that writing the word "Estate" on the beneficiary line of your life insurance application will do the trick. Without further planning, this can create a whole host of headaches for your survivors. Upon your death, life insurance proceeds become available to creditors of your estate. Flowing insurance proceeds through your estate can also increase probate fees or taxes, as well as other estate settlement costs. This is just one example of the problems that can arise when estate planning is neglected or overlooked.

And now for some good news

Although estate planning can be a very complex and involved process, you should not be deterred from taking charge. The information presented in this book, together with the expertise of a proven estate planner, can help you get on side quickly, painlessly, and with minimal expense. All you have to do is make the decision to put a plan in place.

And put those morbid thoughts out of your mind. Estate planning is *not* about death and dying—it's about living with peace of mind.

IN THE NEXT CHAPTER
- Components of an estate plan
- Life, and death, without a plan
- Taxes and more taxes

2

How long is a piece of string?

And other questions you may have

LIFE IS A JIGSAW PUZZLE WITH
MOST OF THE PIECES MISSING.
—Anonymous

Life is one long series of imponderables, of questions that are never truly answered—at least not to our total satisfaction. It may be a cliché, but it is true that the two things that we can count on are death and taxes. Ironically, they are two of the main players on the estate planning stage.

I'm sure there are a lot of other things we can bet the house on, too. Wash the car, and it will probably rain. Answer the phone, and the doorbell will ring. You get the picture.

Nevertheless, life is a bit of a gamble, and you have no choice but to play the cards you're dealt. You can't control everything, but you can take away some of the uncertainty by putting an estate plan into action.

Essentially, estate planning picks up where financial planning ends. It ensures that you are able to maintain and pass on what you've accumulated during your lifetime.

What type of plan is right for you? Well, it's a little like the title of this chapter—and it's not a question this book, or any other, can answer. Every person, every family, and every situation is different. There is no one-size-fits-all solution. Your estate plan must be tailor-fitted to your specific requirements.

Measuring that string

Your estate plan may require some or all of the following components:

- wills
- powers of attorney
- family trusts
- insurance
- charitable gifting programs
- estate freezes
- buy-sell agreements (if you are a small business owner)
- living wills
- funeral/memorial plans

All of these elements can be combined and used to maintain and enhance the value of your estate. Estate planning should be an integrated strategy designed to take care of business both while you are alive and after you've parted company from the rest of us.

So how do you begin? How do you find out the exact length of that string, and discover what will work for you? You've already taken the first step—educating yourself on the basics of estate planning.

The second step will be finding a competent and trusted estate planner who can determine the best options for your particular plan. Someone who will also help you update and modify your estate plan as needed. How do you find such a person? I'll discuss that in Chapter 11.

Forget the Grim Reaper—the taxman cometh

Before we examine the elements involved in developing an estate plan, let's take a brief look at what could happen if you *don't* have some precautionary provisions in place.

Most individuals are aware that Canada does not have estate taxes or succession duties. This leads us to think that we won't get taxed upon death. This couldn't be further from the truth. Let's face it, if the government can tax you while you're still standing up, just imagine what can happen when you're lying down.

If you and your spouse own a home, for example, it's usually deemed your principal residence. You get to keep the proceeds from the sale of the property, unless the banks still have a finger in the pie. Now, if you have a second home that you are renting out, this property is classified as depreciable capital property. When a person dies holding capital property—and the deceased's name is the only one that appears on the deed—Canada Customs and Revenue Agency (CCRA), once known as Revenue Canada, will come calling. And quickly.

Canadian tax law will treat the deceased as if he or she had sold that rental property immediately before death at fair market value. This will trigger the realization of any capital gains (or losses) immediately before death. Translation—a potentially huge tax hit for the deceased's estate.

Since this property was used to generate income through rent, and the individual can claim a deduction for depreciation, there may also be an income inclusion if the property is worth more than its depreciated value immediately before death. Through a tax provision called "recapture of capital cost allowance," the deceased's estate may be required to pay tax on the amount of depreciation that was claimed while the person was alive. The tax take then becomes even more substantial.

A properly prepared estate plan would contain arrangements to transfer the rental property to the surviving spouse or a qualifying trust. There would be no taxation of capital gains or recapture upon the death of the individual. Instead, the "deemed sale" of the property is delayed and takes place upon the death of the surviving spouse (or the actual disposition of the rental property).

The same rules apply to a business that is not passed to the surviving spouse. If everything is left to chance, the deceased's interest in the business is deemed disposed of (sold) and the ever vigilant staff at CCRA will want their cut. And since the business has not really been sold to anyone, coming up with the tax money on its perceived value could be quite a difficult and unpleasant task.

Can we have some more?

These days, many middle-class Canadians who own their own homes also have a family cottage, cabin, or chalet. Once upon a time, CCRA allowed a married couple to have two principal residences, as long as one spouse had the deed to one of the properties and the other spouse had the deed to the other.

This worked nicely for Canadians with a home in the city and a recreational property at the lake or on the ski slopes. That all changed about 20 years ago. Only one property can now be designated as the principal residence by a married couple.

Things can get even more complicated if you rent out the cottage, cabin, or chalet several times a year, and claim depreciation against your tax bill. Again, without the appropriate planning, this second property can leave your estate with a sizable tax bill.

Another area ripe for the picking by the tax department is your RRSP. The tax treatment of RRSPs upon death is somewhat similar to other types of property. If a beneficiary other than your spouse or certain dependent children is named in the RRSP documentation, the retirement plan is deemed collapsed and the tax bite could be devastating.

A lot of people think their RRSPs are not taxable when they die, even though they've benefited from tax deductions when deposits were made and a tax deferral on generated income. It may come as quite a shock to learn that your estate could have a tax bill in the tens or hundreds of thousands of dollars just because you were successful in contributing to your RRSP. More about handling this situation in Chapter 4.

I could go on highlighting potential hazards to your estate if proper planning has not been addressed, but let's get one thing straight: estate planning is *not* about finding a way to cheat the government out of its tax revenues. It *is* about using legitimate, government-sanctioned tax-planning strategies to ensure that you and your survivors do not pay out more than is legally required.

IN THE NEXT CHAPTER
- All about wills
- What happens to those who are intestate
- Guardians for your children
- Handling your assets
- Putting your will to work
- All about trustees
- How to bequeath
- Beneficiaries who are minors
- All about probate
- Privacy and business issues

3

Intestate is not the highway to Florida

All it takes is a little "will power"

THE ART OF LIVING IS MORE LIKE
THAT OF WRESTLING THAN OF
DANCING. THE MAIN THING IS TO
STAND FIRM AND BE READY FOR AN
UNFORESEEN ATTACK.
—Marcus Aurelius

When asked by the governor if he had any last requests, James W. Rodgers, a convict about to face the firing squad, retorted, "Why yes, a bulletproof vest." Despite Rodgers's jovial poke-in-the-eye at capital punishment, his response pretty well sums up the human approach to dealing with issues.

We tend to be reactive rather than proactive. A "Cross that bridge when you come to it" mentality is ingrained in the psyche of the species. The Scouting movement appears to be one of the few exceptions—they strive to "Be prepared."

Even major corporations and government bodies, despite what their public relations people say, are always playing a game of catch-up, scurrying to deal with some sudden crisis. Very few organizations (which, of course, are run by people) have the consistent discipline to anticipate potential problems and head them off at the pass.

Being of sound mind and body

Granted, it's hard to foresee many of the things that are destined to come our way. But there are some handy tools that you can use to deal with the vagaries of life. In estate planning, the most important of these tools is the will. It is the glue that holds all of the other parts together.

Drawing up a will, thinking about a will, or talking about a will are all activities that make many people uncomfortable. Maybe it's the thought of having to deal with a lawyer, but it probably has more to do with our general avoidance of the topic of death. The denial gene kicks in again.

There is nothing complicated about drawing up a will, although many wills can be complex documents. It's as simple as going to your lawyer, and providing personal and family details. Most lawyers are aware of what information they have to collect from you and will be thorough in putting what you need in place.

An even better approach, especially if you must consider a lot of factors—owning a business, substantial financial assets, a load of dependents—is to meet with an estate planner before dealing with your lawyer. In fact, just about every estate planner has a lawyer he or she can access to assist in will preparation.

A lawyer will typically spend about four to five hours working on even the most simple of wills. This includes at least one meeting with the client to take instructions, the completion of several drafts of the will, and attending to the will's execution (signing and witnessing). Most lawyers usually charge a flat fee of under $500. They are willing to discount the cost of this service because they want to attract new clients and maintain their current clientele. Wills are recognized as the "loss leader" of a lawyer's practice. Lawyers expect that if they do a good job on the will, they will get the legal work associated with winding up the estate.

For those who like the do-it-yourself approach, there are many kits on the market. These may work for individuals with few assets and a relatively simple estate. For the majority of Canadians, however, these self-prepared wills can be a false economy. You may save a few dollars now, but it could cost your estate and your family a whole lot more down the road.

Even drawing up a simple will requires knowledge of complex issues such as taxes upon death, the appointment of executors and trustees, guardians for minor children, disposal of assets, and bequests to charitable organizations. It's best to leave it to the experts.

No will? No way

Some of the queasiness people feel when they think about preparing their will is due to the terminology. Let's face it, nobody likes to read the fine print on contracts, insurance policies, and the like. It's intimidating. What you may interpret one way could mean something totally different in the world of accountants, lawyers, and insurance companies.

Don't let the big legal words daunt you. They usually mean something quite simple. For example, the term "intestate." Though some people claim they've driven on one travelling through the United States, the term simply means that someone has passed on without leaving a valid will. Intestate—no will.

A simple meaning, but a very risky state of affairs. What happens if someone dies intestate? Plenty. And not much of it would be to your liking.

Executor choice

One of the main purposes of a will is to appoint an executor. The executor has the power to deal with the deceased's estate and will ultimately distribute the assets to the beneficiaries under the will. Ideally, this person would be a family member or close friend, and someone who agrees to this appointment.

If you die without a will, someone will have to go to court to be appointed as "administrator" of your estate. Usually, this is a family member. However, the court has the discretion to appoint someone else to administer the estate if it makes sense.

A huge pitfall of not having a will is the time it takes to appoint an administrator. A long delay could result in losses to the estate, especially if there are assets such as stocks or real estate that cannot be properly managed before the appointment of the administrator.

The other big consideration is that the court-appointed person may not have been your first choice. The court may require the administrator to post a bond to ensure that the estate is reimbursed in the event that mismanagement occurs.

From there, things can get even uglier. The provincial government also gets a say in who gets what from your estate. Each province has rules governing the distribution of an estate where there is no will. Although the provincial governments have tried to be reasonable in their approach, these rules won't necessarily reflect your wishes.

How bad can it get?

Let's look at an example of what can occur when someone dies without leaving a will. Frank, who always meant to put his final wishes down on paper, dies suddenly in an automobile accident. The will he was getting around to making just didn't happen.

He is survived by his wife and two children, and leaves an estate worth $400,000 after all liabilities have been paid. Under the intestacy rules in Ontario, Frank's wife is entitled to the first $200,000 of estate value. She and the two children would share the remaining $200,000 equally, with the children not receiving their share until they reach the age of majority.

This seems nice and tidy on the surface, but Frank had other wishes, too. He wanted to help out his elderly parents and make some token bequests to his nieces and nephews. As a result of the intestacy rules, these wishes will not be fulfilled.

Also, because of the type of property in his estate, the gifts to his children may not be very tax effective. Any capital property that did not go to Frank's spouse was deemed to be disposed of at fair market value, triggering the taxation of accumulated gains. Moreover, even at the age of majority, the children may not be mature enough to properly deal with a significant inheritance.

These days, a larger segment of the population lives common law than ever before. If Frank and his wife were not legally wed, the situation could get even more complicated.

In most provinces, common-law spouses are not treated as spouses for purposes of the intestacy rules. As a result, they would not receive any property under these rules. However, they may have a property claim under certain trust principles if they contributed to the acquisition of, or improvement to, property owned by the deceased. They may also be able to make a claim for maintenance and support against the assets of the estate. More wrangling and headaches all around.

This, of course, may change in the near future as provincial governments come up to speed and react appropriately to recognize this aspect of Canadian family life.

It is also important to note that the intestacy rules may be overridden by other provincial legislation. In Ontario, for instance, a spouse can make a claim for a share of the "net family property" existing at the date of death. And certain other provinces protect the surviving spouse's interest in the family home. Things can get complicated pretty quickly.

What's in it for the kids?

When minor children are involved, the layers of complications increase. If an infant is a beneficiary of the estate, his or her share must be managed by the Public Trustee (a court appointed public servant) unless someone else is appointed by the court as guardian for the property of that child.

That child will become entitled to his or her share of the estate upon attaining the age of majority, even though that person may not be mature enough to manage those funds at that time.

If there is no surviving spouse, the court will need to appoint a guardian to look after the child until he or she reaches the age of majority. The person appointed as guardian may not be someone the deceased would have selected.

A quick recap

It's clearly difficult to argue against the benefits of having a will. Your will

- allows you (the testator if you are male, testatrix if you are female—don't allow the legalese to confuse you) to select the person who will take care of distributing your estate;
- ensures that the estate assets are directed to the people you want to benefit;
- allows you to make special provisions for infant children and create special trusts for their benefit;
- speeds up the administration of the estate, and can reduce taxes and other costs that might otherwise arise.

Now that you recognize how important it is to have a properly drafted will, the next stage is to take a look at your worldly goods and figure out where they will go when you do.

Covering your assets

What to do with your assets is probably one of the most important decisions to make as you put your last will and testament to paper. The first step is to determine the nature, type, and value of assets that will form part of the estate. This will often influence the terms and provisions of the will.

Certain assets will flow outside of the estate and cannot be gifted under your will. For example, real estate held in "joint tenancy" with another person will be transferred automatically to that other person. In other words, if you and your spouse both have your names on the deed to your home, your spouse will become sole owner, no questions asked. The home is not part of the estate, and as such, there will be no probate fees (we'll get to that on page 33) or other estate administration costs. If, however, you own property with another person as "tenants in common," each person is assumed to own an equal interest in the property. Upon death, your interest in that property will fall into your estate and be governed by the terms of your will. If you own real estate with your spouse, a business partner, or someone else, it is important to determine the type of ownership.

Similarly, insurance proceeds will be paid directly to a named beneficiary—for example, your spouse—and will not be considered part of the estate. The same is generally true for RRSPs with a named beneficiary. As a result, these assets should be excluded in determining the size of the estate. It is a good idea to review the beneficiary designations under your insurance and registered plans. You want to ensure that the proceeds are going to a named beneficiary and not your estate. You also want to confirm that the proceeds are going to the right person, particularly if you have divorced or there have been other changes in family circumstances since you set up the plans.

Business assets may be subject to a buy-sell arrangement that takes effect upon death. This is often the case with shares in private corporations or partnership interests. The executor of the estate will complete the sale of these business interests and will distribute the cash or promissory note to the named beneficiaries.

A note of caution for those with assets outside of the country. If, for example, you own a condominium in Florida, it is advisable to have a separate will that meets the requirements of that state's legislation. This will ensure that the property can be liquidated or transferred to the beneficiaries on a timely basis with minimal costs. There may also be tax issues in the foreign jurisdiction that need to be considered by an estate planner that is familiar with the rules of that country or state.

The best person to ensure that your assets are integrated into the will in the most effective manner is your estate planner, working hand in hand with your lawyer.

Making your will work

All wills include a clause that states that the deceased revokes all prior wills and codicils (a legal term for a supplement to an existing will containing changes and additions). Don't fret; your lawyer will include it as a matter of course. This inclusion will ensure that your current will is the only one that governs the distribution of your estate. Routine stuff, but quite necessary.

Executors and trustees

Your executor has a number of responsibilities, including arranging the funeral, obtaining court approval of the will (known as "probating the will") if required, paying creditors, administering the assets, and ensuring the distribution of assets to the named beneficiaries.

When you are dealing with a simple estate, the appointment of the executor is fairly straightforward. If the client is married and the spouse is the main beneficiary, the surviving spouse is normally appointed as the executor of the will.

If your spouse has predeceased you, then the next logical choice would be one or more of your children, if you have them. If you name only one of your children, you may want to consider appointing a trust company as coexecutor. In the event of disputes, the trust company can act as a buffer between the child appointed executor and his or her siblings.

A trust company is also useful in cases where trusts have been established for grandchildren or other beneficiaries. These trusts could last for decades, and it is useful to have a company in place to perform most of the administrative work and ensure continuity.

A trust company can bring an extensive range of expertise to the management of certain types of assets that are to be held in trust. If you have business assets or rental property that you want to hold in trust, you can appoint a trust company to properly administer these assets. It is important to notify the company in advance and determine the fees they will charge for this service. These may be significant, but the work involved in administering the estate can be as well. Depending on the size of the estate, these fees may be negotiable.

Trustee powers

How do you make sure that your appointed trustee works in the best interest of your estate and the provisions of your will? As with most other areas affecting us, the government lends a hand. When it comes to managing the assets in an estate, certain provinces—including Ontario, Manitoba, Prince Edward Island, and Nova Scotia—have a simple requirement that trustees invest in a "prudent" manner.

However, other provinces, such as British Columbia, currently have trust legislation that specifies the investment powers of trustees. In these provinces, trustees are limited to more conservative investments, such as:

- federal, provincial, and municipal government securities
- first mortgages on real estate in Canada
- bank deposits and term deposits in a credit union

You can expand or reduce these investment powers under your will. For example, you could grant very broad investment powers by stating that the trustee is not limited to investments authorized by provincial legislation. You could also indicate that certain "permitted" investments are *not* to be made by the trustee.

How do you determine the types of investment powers that your trustee should be granted under a will? One consideration is the investment expertise of the appointed individual. If the executor has considerable experience with different types of investments, you may want to provide expanded investment powers. On the other hand, if he or she is somewhat unsophisticated in financial matters, you may want to limit the types of investments or allow the delegation of investment decisions to designated investment advisers. Another option is to appoint a coexecutor to assist with investment decisions.

It is also important for you to inform your estate planner and lawyer about the type of investments you currently hold. If you own shares in a small business, the retention or sale of those shares should be addressed in the will. If your trustee is expected to continue to hold those shares, this should be explicitly set out in the will.

The trustee should also be given the power to vote those shares and act as a director of the company. Furthermore, if you want the trustees to have the power to purchase insurance policies on the lives of the beneficiaries, this should be set out in the will.

Other powers

Remember, it's your will and you can do want you want—within reason, that is. After all, this was undertaken while of sound mind and body. If, working with your advisers, you see fit to include additional investment powers, then exercise that right.

For example, if you have mutual and segregated funds in your investment portfolio, you can use your will to allow the executor/trustee to hold onto these assets or replace them with similar assets. The executor/trustee can also consult with investment advisers, with reasonable fees being paid from estate assets.

There are other types of powers that you might want to grant your trustee under your will. These powers could include the ability of the trustee to make contributions to a spousal RRSP, make certain elections and designations under the Income Tax Act to save the estate taxes, and distribute funds on behalf of a minor beneficiary to that person's legal guardian.

Giving it all away

Remembering others upon your death is usually accommodated in two different parts of your will. The first part sets out specific gifts of property and cash, while the next part deals with the remainder of your estate, commonly referred to as the "residue."

In the first section you can allocate personal items—such as the family home, the cottage, jewelry, and family heirlooms—to specific people. You can itemize any bequest to a favourite charity. This is also where you describe any trusts you may wish to set up, usually for grandchildren or perhaps for an adult child who requires special care for physical or mental disabilities.

The second section deals with the residue of your estate. This is what is left over after the creditors have been paid, all probate fees and other estate administration expenses have been taken care of, and specific bequests have been made to named beneficiaries. The "residuary" beneficiaries could include your spouse, your children, or a charitable organization. It is a catch-all provision to make sure that there is nothing left in your estate when all is said and done.

When determining who gets what, you will need to consider what happens if an intended beneficiary passes away before you do. Your lawyer will normally include a provision that contemplates a beneficiary predeceasing you. If, for example, an adult child passes away before you do, your will could provide that the bequest goes to the original beneficiary's children.

As mentioned earlier, in matters such as this, one size does not fit all. These types of provisions can accommodate a response to just about any situation. That's why a will is such a powerful and flexible tool.

But remember, the amount of money you intend to leave to your beneficiaries can depend on several variables. If you live longer than you or your relatives expect, you could use up a significant amount of your assets, which reduces what is available to your beneficiaries.

Also, all taxes and estate administration expenses must be paid before calculating the beneficiaries' share of the estate. Proper planning and professional guidance is vital to ensure that your wishes are carried out.

Guardians for minor children

In preparing your will, you must make special provisions for minor children. For your own peace of mind, you must be dispassionate and examine the potential fallout if both parents are lost in a common disaster, such as a traffic accident.

The first step is to consider whom you would like to act as a guardian to your surviving children. Don't forget to discuss this role with the potential guardian and get his or her agreement to act in this capacity, since that person can decline to act.

Naming a guardian does not automatically ensure that the person will have this role. The guardian named must apply to the court to be appointed as permanent guardian. The court can refuse the appointment of a guardian if it doesn't believe the appointment is in the best interests of the children.

The guardian should have both the maturity and energy to take care of the children, possibly over an extended period of time.

It might be necessary to provide financial assistance through the will so the guardian can purchase a new home or upgrade the current home to accommodate the children's needs.

Minor beneficiaries

If a minor is appointed as a beneficiary under a will, the gift normally has to be transferred to a government official commonly referred to as the Public Trustee. However, a family member could apply to the court to be appointed guardian of the property for the minor beneficiary. The Public Trustee or appointed guardian would administer the gift and invest any cash in very conservative investments.

The minor beneficiary would become entitled to the proceeds of the gift upon attaining the age of majority, which is either age 18 or 19 in most provinces. I don't know if you can remember what your financial priority was at that age, but mine was to save enough money to buy a new Mustang. I certainly didn't have the maturity to deal with a large amount of money then. Neither do most other young people.

One of the best ways to address this issue is by establishing a trust for the minor beneficiaries. A commonplace arrangement is to distribute the trust property in two stages—for example, half at age 21 and the remainder at age 25.

You can, however, stipulate that the trustee, at his or her discretion, can make earlier payments to the parents of the child (if it's your grandchild), or to the guardian of your child, for "care and maintenance." This way, you can ensure that the day-to-day expenses and educational costs are covered while postponing the payment of any large sums of money until the child is older.

Probate fees and facts

"Probate" is another legal term that means something very simple but requires thoughtful consideration. What is it? Probate is when your executor goes to court to confirm that you have passed away, he or she has been properly appointed, and there is no other will that governs your estate. Once your will is probated, a third party can then be assured that the executor has the power to deal with the estate assets.

Simple enough, except that it costs money—often quite a sizable chunk of your assets. Provincial governments levy "probate fees or taxes" that are supposed to approximate the court costs involved in probating the will. These fees are normally a percentage of the value of the estate.

Unfortunately, several provinces, including Ontario, Nova Scotia, and British Columbia, recently decided that probate fees were an attractive way to raise additional tax revenues. Those provinces have essentially tripled their fees in the past few years.

What probate will cost you from sea to sea

Province	Probate Fees/Taxes
British Columbia	No fee under $25,000; $25,000–$50,000: $6 per $1,000; over $50,000: $14 per $1,000; no maximum fee.
Alberta	Progressive rates start at $25 for the first $10,000, increasing to a maximum of $400 for estates in excess of $1 million.
Saskatchewan	$7 per $1,000; no maximum fee.
Manitoba	$50 for the first $10,000; over $10,000: $50 plus $6 per $1,000 thereafter; no maximum fee.
Ontario	$5 per $1,000 for the first $50,000; $15 per $1,000 thereafter; no maximum fee.
Quebec	No probate fees for notarial wills.
New Brunswick	Graduated flat fees up to $100 for estates up to $20,000; $5 per $1,000 for estates worth more than $20,000; no maximum fee.
Prince Edward Island	Progressive rates starting at $50 for the first $10,000, increasing to $400 for estates of $100,000 and $400 plus $4 per $1,000 thereafter; no maximum fee.
Nova Scotia	Graduated flat fees up to $700 for estates up to $100,000; for estates over $100,000, the fee is $700 plus $12 per $1,000; no maximum fee.
Newfoundland	$60 for the first $1,000; $5 per $1,000 thereafter; no maximum fee.

A new wrinkle in probate fees

For a while, it looked like we were going to get a bit of a break. A recent decision by the Supreme Court of Canada held that the probate fees levied in Ontario were unconstitutional. Essentially, the Supreme Court determined that probate fees represent a direct tax and have to be approved by the provincial legislature.

Since Ontario's probate fees have been set by government regulation since 1950, the Supreme Court held that they were not properly enacted. While this decision only concerned probate fees in Ontario, it will apply to any province that has set their probate fees by regulation.

Does this mean that you don't have to worry about probate fees any more? Unfortunately not. The Ontario government recently passed the Estate Administration Tax Act that imposes an "estate tax" to replace probate fees. This legislation is retroactive to 1950 and mirrors the probate fee rates that existed under the old system.

Most of the other affected provinces have also followed suit by passing new legislation. For all practical purposes, nothing has really changed. Now we have estate taxes instead of probate fees in most provinces.

Is probate really necessary?

Not all wills need to obtain probate from the court. It all depends on the type of assets in the estate. For example, if the estate is fairly simple and consists of personal property and small accounts at financial institutions, it may be possible to avoid probate.

But estates that include real estate or shares in public companies will normally need to be probated. In Quebec, however, probate is not required if the will is prepared by a notary under notarial seal.

A wrinkle of another kind

One big problem with probate is that the will and a complete description of the estate's contents must be filed with the court. From there, it becomes a matter of public record.

What does that mean to you? It means that the media and members of the public can have access to very personal, and often confidential, information relating to estate assets and beneficiaries. All a person has to do is pay a small fee to the court, and they can get complete access to your will and a list of your assets.

Fortunately, there are a number of planning strategies that can be used to minimize the concerns around probate and the confidentiality of your will. The simplest is to gift assets to intended beneficiaries prior to death. Of course, you may not want to part with your titanium golf clubs or Jaguar XKE ahead of your demise. It's a tough call.

Another planning technique involves the transfer of assets into joint tenancy with a spouse (including common law spouses) or another family member. As discussed previously, assets held in joint tenancy will pass automatically to the other joint tenant upon death. These assets do not go through the estate and, as a result, are not subject to probate. Some caution should prevail, though, as you can trigger taxes when you transfer capital assets that have appreciated in value into joint tenancy with someone other than your spouse.

You can also avoid probate costs by naming your beneficiaries under your RRSPs. These funds will be paid directly to your beneficiaries. The same would be true if you purchased an insurance policy and named your spouse, children, or grandchildren as beneficiaries. This would be a very effective method of transferring large sums of capital to family members without paying probate fees.

Opportunities for business owners

Small business owners can also benefit from some of these planning techniques. Shares in a private corporation often represent a significant asset. If those shares flow through the owner's estate, it could result in the payment of higher probate fees or taxes than necessary.

The transfer of shares in a private corporation does not usually require that the will be probated. A recent Ontario court decision has confirmed that it is possible to establish a separate will that only deals with the shares in a private corporation. This will would not require probate; therefore, no fees would be payable on this part of the estate's assets.

The business owner may also have personal debt related to the acquisition of investments. This debt does not reduce the value of the investments for probate purposes. If the investments and associated debt were transferred into the private holding company, only the net amount would be included in the share value of the business.

Here's how it works. Suppose someone dies owning investments worth $600,000, and there was bank debt of $400,000 related to the acquisition of those investments. Probate fees would be calculated on the full $600,000.

If the investments and debt were transferred to a holding company, however, the value of the corporation would only increase by $200,000. Thus, the size of the estate for probate purposes could be reduced by $400,000, which is equal to the amount of the debt relating to the investments. Of course, the cost of setting up and maintaining the corporation must be considered. Also, the ownership of investments within a private corporation could have negative tax consequences that need to be considered.

When not to avoid probate fees

There are other issues that need to be considered when using probate avoidance techniques. For example:
- you may not want to give up control of the assets by gifting them away or transferring them into joint ownership;
- there may be significant transaction costs associated with the transfer of property, including legal and accounting fees, real

estate commissions, land transfer tax, goods and services tax (GST), and capital gains taxes.

As with anything else involving your assets and other valuables, your professional advisers should be involved in preparing a thorough cost/benefit analysis to see what strategy makes the most sense.

IN THE NEXT CHAPTER
- The under-utilized RRSP
- Spousal RRSPs
- Separation and divorce issues
- Splitting income
- Forms of income
- Tax friendly income
- Integrating insurance
- Accessing your cash
- The holding company option

4

What we need is a plan

Don't get taxed to the max while building your estate

THE WAY TO CRUSH THE
BOURGEOISIE IS TO GRIND
THEM BETWEEN MILLSTONES OF
TAXATION AND INFLATION.
—Vladimir Ilyich Lenin

While Vladimir Ilyich Lenin implemented his political agenda in czarist Russia, democratic nations across the world also adopted the practice of "grinding" their citizens with often overwhelming tax burdens.

Taxes are a curse, but, like our governments, we have to learn to live with them. Most governments are quite creative when it comes to finding new and ingenious ways to increase revenues through fiscal policy.

The general public, on the other hand, is generally uninformed about the ways that they can legally reduce and defer their tax load. They believe that only the very wealthy can make use of tax breaks and loopholes. As far as middle-class Canadians go, Lenin might as well be in power.

Estate planning is about preserving and transferring your worldly goods to your beneficiaries. The world of taxation can have a significant impact on building and preserving your estate. Most Canadians should be more active in exploring ways to reduce the amount of tax they pay, both over their lifetimes and beyond the grave.

Canada's under-utilized tax shelter

One of the easiest, most effective ways to save on taxes in this country is the Registered Retirement Savings Plan, or RRSP.

An RRSP is a simple enough concept. Every year, you can deposit funds into an RRSP up to a certain limit—usually 18 percent of the previous year's earned income to a maximum annual contribution of $13,500. Contributions made by yourself or your employer into a company-sponsored registered pension plan will reduce the maximum allowable contribution. In exchange for your yearly contribution, the government will provide you with a reduction in your taxes. For example, if you put $8,000 into your RRSP in 2000, and your marginal tax rate was 40 percent, your taxes would be reduced by about $3,200. In addition, your RRSP assets are allowed to grow in value without annual tax until you begin to receive income under your RRSP or you attain the age of 69.

Not a bad deal. Firstly, you save on your annual taxes. Secondly, you can compound your assets without taxation until age 69, when your plan must be collapsed or converted to a Registered Retirement Income Fund (RRIF) or registered payout annuity. And thirdly, you are building up a significant amount of retirement assets and a potentially sizable estate.

Granted, your RRSP is not a total tax eliminator. It merely defers taxes until you take the money out of the plan. But remember, assets outside of your plan are subject to annual taxes and would never grow as quickly or to the same degree. As well, you may be in a lower tax bracket when you start receiving the payments under your RRSP.

Paying some tax later in life is a small price to pay for the tax-free compounding your assets will enjoy now. Surprisingly, the majority of us do not flex this tax-saving muscle. In any given year, only about a third of all Canadians who are eligible to do so make an RRSP contribution. Even more surprising, of the individuals who do contribute, only about 10 percent actually make the maximum contribution.

Flex that RRSP muscle

If you are concerned about your financial future, as well as that of your children and grandchildren, one of your best strategies is to maximize your annual RRSP contributions. If you can't, the government will allow you to "catch up" on your unused RRSP contribution room in subsequent years.

Don't have the cash? Many financial institutions will provide a loan for a catch-up contribution, usually at a favourable interest rate. When you get your refund—and it should be a fairly nice sum—you can use it to help pay down the loan. The interest paid is more than offset by the tax-deferred gains that these additional contributions will be earning.

Not just another pretty face

Did you know that your spouse can help reduce your tax bill now and in retirement? Aren't you glad you got married?

In many households, one person earns more than the other. In this case, the higher wage earner has more RRSP contribution room and, as a result, the ability to accumulate substantially more money in his or her RRSP.

Assuming the higher wage earner maximized their contributions, he or she would receive considerably more retirement income. This would likely put him or her in a higher marginal tax bracket than the spouse at retirement time.

To remedy this situation, the higher wage earner should make contributions to an RRSP owned by his or her spouse until their RRSPs are comparable in size. The lower wage earner receives a boost to his or her RRSP assets, while the higher wage earner can still claim the tax deduction. This spousal RRSP strategy can be quite effective in reducing a couple's overall tax bill on retirement.

The catch? The money must remain in the lower earner's plan for three years. If the spouse cashes out any portion of the RRSP before that time, the tax hit will be attributed back to the higher-earning spouse. In addition, the higher wage earner cannot contribute more than their own annual personal contribution limit. For example, if he or she has contribution room of $10,000, then that person has the choice of contributing all or a portion of this total amount to a spousal RRSP.

Separation is not just an issue for the Parti Québécois

Many couples are actively using the spousal RRSP approach in their retirement planning. But some refuse to consider this strategy because they are concerned over what would happen in the event of a separation or divorce.

What people don't realize is that, in most provinces, the value of RRSPs and all other property accumulated while married will normally be equally divided between spouses on separation or divorce. It doesn't matter who owns the RRSP or who made the contribution, the total accumulation is split in half. Given this approach, it makes little sense to avoid taking advantage of spousal RRSP contributions.

A split of a different kind

Another consideration for dual income families is the way that expenses are split. Quite often the higher wage earner will take on the bulk of the living expenses, such as the mortgage, insurance, property taxes, and car payments.

But the lower wage earner might pick up the costs of groceries, other household expenses, and maybe even the odd vacation, leaving that person with little cash for investing. At the same time, the higher earner might have money left over to invest.

What couples like this need to realize is that their earnings can be a mutual pool of money. If the higher earner picks up more of the costs and allows the lower earner to invest his or her residual cash, that investment will be taxed at the lower wage earner's tax rate. The savings could be substantial and could be reinvested to further their joint financial security.

Allocating more of the family expenses to the spouse in the higher tax bracket to free up investment funds for the lower taxed spouse is a fairly simple and effective strategy for reducing taxes. But similar strategies involving the transfer of investments and other property to the lower income spouse can create problems.

Complications are possible

Putting investments in the hands of the spouse in the lower marginal tax bracket makes sense. It provides an overall tax savings to the family. However, to prevent this loss of tax revenue, the federal government has enacted the "income attribution rules."

These rules take up about 10 pages of the Income Tax Act and are very complicated. But the main rules can generally be summarized as follows:

- If a spouse transfers or lends property to another spouse, the income from that property must be included in the income of the transferor spouse.
- If a parent transfers property to a minor child, the income from that property will be included in the parent's income until the child attains the age of 18. However, the rules applicable to minor children do not apply to capital gains. It is possible, therefore, to "income split" with a minor child when the property generates capital gains (like an equity mutual fund or stock investment).

The bottom line is to take care when transferring any investment property to your spouse or children. Run it by your accountant, adviser, lawyer, or financial planner to determine who will be responsible for future taxes.

Forms of investment that reduce taxes

Some of you will look back with affection at the early 1980s, when your investments benefited from sky-high interest rates brought on by out-of-control inflation. Those were the days. While Canada Savings Bonds (CSBs) and guaranteed investment certificates were paying out solid interest returns, rampant double-digit inflation was eroding the disposable income of most Canadians.

Times have changed. While these types of investments are still providing returns close to the rate of inflation, inflation is now hovering at an annual rate of 2 to 3 percent. Even rising gasoline prices have not seriously affected Canada's inflation rate. And since investment income is always taxed more heavily than other forms, the returns on these investments have dwindled.

As a result, many individuals have shifted away from GICs and similar interest-paying financial products, and put their funds into the stock market and mutual funds sectors.

Better returns and less tax exposure

While the primary advantage of equity investing is higher rates of return, individuals can also receive some tax benefits from these types of investments.

With interest-bearing investments, interest income must be reported annually, even if it's not received. Taxes are then paid at your marginal tax rate—unless you had the foresight to stash your GICs or CSBs in your RRSP. For those in the top marginal tax bracket, the government takes close to half of the interest. The rest is slowly eroded by inflation.

With equity investments, on the other hand, only a percentage of the capital growth is included in income. This inclusion rate has now dropped to 50 percent for dispositions of property occurring after October 28, 2000. So even if you could earn the same rate of return on a GIC as the growth rate of an equity investment, you would still be better off with the equity investment on an after-tax basis.

Another advantage is that you normally only pay tax on capital gains on the sale of the appreciated investment—even if this investment is outside of an RRSP. So if you hold onto your shares, or the mutual fund has a long-term hold strategy, you can avoid paying tax on accumulating gains over an extended period of time. This can create additional tax savings over interest-bearing investments, plus better compounding of the returns.

Of course, equity investments are more risky than GICs, and there is the potential for negative growth. However, if you purchase quality stocks or mutual funds with a strong track record and hold on to them for the long term, you can minimize that risk.

Dividends are also tax friendly

Dividend income from Canadian companies is treated differently than interest income and capital gains. For example, an investor receiving $1,000 in dividends has to include $1,250 in income when filing his or her tax return. In other words, the dividend is "grossed up" by 25 percent.

Can the government be so starved for money that it will tax you on what you haven't earned? Not really. The federal government also provides you with a dividend tax credit equal to 16⅔ percent of the grossed up amount. After taking into account provincial taxes, this reduces the actual tax burden on dividends to about 36 percent for someone who otherwise pays tax at a 50 percent tax rate.

It may seem a strange way to do things, but the government has a pretty good reason for assessing dividends this way. Like individuals, companies pay tax on their net business income. So when a company pays out dividends, they are paid from its after-tax profits. Since the company has already paid one level of tax on this income, the federal government did not feel it would be fair to levy a tax at full rates when the income is distributed to shareholders in the form of dividends.

To take into account the corporate tax that has already been paid, the dividend is increased to represent the before-tax earnings of the company paying the dividend. The shareholder is then given a credit to offset the tax already paid at the corporate level.

Dividend income can be particularly attractive to individuals with little other taxable income. Depending on the province of residence, the dividend tax credit can be used to offset the tax payable on dividend income up to about $22,000.

Insure yourself against tax

Insurance can play a significant role in your estate plan, providing your loved ones with the financial resources to carry on. Insurance can also be used to reduce and/or defer your tax bill.

With the purchase of an exempt insurance policy, the cash value can accumulate on a tax-deferred basis. How? In essence, a policyholder can accumulate cash within an exempt contract, and investment earnings will not be subject to tax as long as the funds remain in the contract.

This not only makes insurance an important estate planning tool, but also a very attractive investment vehicle. If you try to withdraw the cash from the policy, however, any investment gains will become taxable. In that sense, it works somewhat like an RRSP. Fortunately, there are strategies that permit you to withdraw your accumulated income from an insurance policy on a tax effective basis.

Insure your peace of mind

Insurance is often given short shrift when individuals or couples try to figure out a financial plan for themselves. However, insurance can be quite a flexible and valuable tool. The key is to understand how insurance works and find out what type best suits your needs.

There are many different types of life insurance policies, but the two main categories are term insurance and permanent insurance.

Term insurance provides coverage for a limited period of time. You can get term insurance for one year, for five years, for 10 years, or to age 75. These policies can usually be renewed at regular intervals, although the premium goes up as the applicant grows older.

Term policies can normally be converted to permanent insurance without medical evidence. However, there are age limits for both renewing and converting a term policy. You would normally purchase term insurance to cover financial needs with a fixed duration—the repayment of a residential mortgage, for example.

A lot of people with permanent insurance needs will purchase term insurance because it is less expensive. They can invest the premium savings and get a much better return. If they do a good job with their investments, they figure they won't need insurance when they retire.

For many people, especially individuals with young families and mortgages, term insurance is likely the best solution, especially in the short run. But the premiums for term insurance increase at the end of each term and the costs can become prohibitive.

Also, if you convert a term policy into a permanent policy, the insurance charges will reflect the older age of the individual. For these reasons, if the need for insurance is long term—to cover tax liabilities upon death, for example—permanent insurance is the way to go.

A permanent solution

Few people are aware of the tax advantages associated with permanent insurance (such as universal life). Often you can do better "investing" within the insurance policy than buying term insurance and investing the difference.

Under a permanent policy, the premium is initially higher than the mortality charges and other expenses. The excess premium is invested by the insurer and creates a cash reserve. In turn, the cash reserve is accumulated to fund future insurance charges. As we mentioned above, this cash reserve accumulates on a tax-deferred basis. So, unlike traditional investments, you can accumulate cash within the policy without the payment of annual tax.

This can often result in the cash value of the policy accumulating to a much higher amount than had the person purchased term insurance and deposited the remainder into a taxable investment.

More flexibility introduced

There are restrictions on the amount you can deposit into an exempt insurance policy. In addition to having to qualify medically for the insurance policy, the Income Tax Act imposes limits on how much can be accumulated within a policy on a tax-deferred basis. This is often referred to as the "exempt test limits."

If the policy's values exceed those limits, the accumulating income in the policy is taxed similarly to interest income. But if the policy remains exempt, you can still deposit a fair amount of cash into an insurance policy and benefit from tax-deferred accumulation.

To compete for your investment dollars, most insurance companies have introduced newer generations of universal life policies. These offer a broad range of investment options, including guaranteed accounts, accounts linked to the returns of equity and bond indices, and even prominent mutual funds.

Accessing your cash

Withdrawing funds from an insurance policy may trigger a tax payment on the accumulating income. This is somewhat similar to the tax treatment of RRSP payments. But even taking this into account, an exempt insurance policy can provide an attractive investment return if the funds have been allowed to accumulate for enough time to take advantage of the tax-free compounding.

The payout of a death benefit under an exempt policy is totally tax-free. Unfortunately, the insured party will never directly realize the benefit of this money. He or she has to be content knowing that his or her loved ones will be in good financial shape.

There is one more way that an insured person can access tax-free cash from a policy. And this is something that can be done while he or she is still alive.

Tax-free cash?

Does tax-free cash sound too good to be true? Well, the insurance industry has figured out a way to get at the cash in a policy without triggering tax repercussions. Basically, this strategy uses the policy's cash values as collateral for a line of credit with a bank.

The real kicker is that the bank does not require repayment of the loan or interest until the death of the insured individual. The death benefit is structured so that it increases with the growth of the policy's cash value. Upon the death of the insured, the entire amount of the death benefit—including the policy's cash value—is paid out tax-free to the estate. The estate then uses the death benefit to repay the bank loan plus accumulated interest.

But what about the deceased's estate—doesn't it lose the benefit of the insurance proceeds? Not necessarily. If the arrangement is managed properly, the estate or the named beneficiaries will still get a substantial sum of money. As a result, the policyholder can benefit while he or she is alive, using the cash for investment purposes or for more pressing financial concerns, and still take care of his or her estate planning needs.

One wonders how long this can go on before Canada Customs and Revenue Agency decides to pull the plug on this arrangement.

To date, it looks good for individuals wanting to use this strategy in their financial and estate plans. The insurance companies appear to have done their homework. They have tax opinions on their side, as well as banks lined up to do the lending. These tax opinions confirm that the collateral assignment of the policy is not a disposition of the policy for tax purposes. As a result, there is no tax reporting to the policyholder and the loans represent a tax-free flow of capital.

There has been some discussion about the anti-avoidance rules, but the lawyers providing the tax opinion do not think that CCRA would or could challenge the arrangement on this basis.

A caveat or two

The loan is a fairly typical bank transaction except in two respects. One, the original loan does not have to be repaid until the death of the life-insured party, as long as the loan is in good standing. Two, the bank agrees to lend additional funds to pay the loan interest, as long as the total loan does not exceed a certain percentage of the policy's cash value (ranging from 50 to 95 percent, depending on the underlying investment accounts). In effect, the loan interest is compounded.

Upon the death of the policyholder, the death benefit, which is received tax-free by the estate or beneficiary, will first repay the bank. The program is structured so there still is a considerable death benefit available to go to the designated beneficiaries of the deceased.

Not a bad set-up from a tax-planning perspective. While nothing is 100 percent guaranteed in this world, this strategy will work well for some individuals, based on their particular circumstances.

There are some other issues that should be considered. This strategy should only be used after contributions to the policyholder's RRSP and company pension plan have been maximized. Also, he or she should be in a position where non-deductible debt, such as a residential mortgage or car loan, has been eliminated or at least substantially reduced.

The concept also appears to be highly dependent on assumed mortality ages, as well as interest rates. If the life insured lives too long, the loan may hit the maximum cash value limit and the bank will have to take actions to preserve its security. This could include surrendering the policy, which would have disastrous tax consequences. Also, if the credited interest rate in the policy drops significantly below the loan interest rate charged by the bank, the loan could be called. Therefore, the arrangement must be carefully structured and regularly monitored by the policyholder and the bank to ensure that it is compatible with both parties' requirements.

More things to ponder

Another important aspect of life insurance relates to beneficiary designations. Provincial insurance legislation allows the policyholder to designate one or more beneficiaries to receive the death benefit, and the relationship of the beneficiary to the life insured can have significant implications.

For example, if a spouse or child of the insured person is named as beneficiary, the policy's cash values, as well as the death benefit payable to the beneficiary, is generally exempt from seizure by creditors of the policyholder. This makes life insurance an excellent savings vehicle for professionals, business owners, and other individuals who might be exposed to litigation or other claims by creditors.

If the policyholder is single or widowed, and doesn't have any children, there is a way to ensure protection from creditors. It comes in the form of irrevocable beneficiaries. If you designate a beneficiary irrevocably, you cannot change that designation without the consent of that beneficiary.

Another bonus in naming a beneficiary is that the death benefit flows directly to the named individual and is not included in the deceased's estate for probate purposes. This could significantly reduce probate fees and other expenses otherwise payable by the estate.

Don't be left holding the tax bill

For some people, the use of a holding company is another estate planning option. A holding company may benefit older individuals who own significant non-registered investments, such as term deposits, mutual funds, and stocks and bonds.

For example, let's look at the situation of a 66-year-old divorced man. He has two children in their 30s, and his will gives everything to them when he dies. He is quite wealthy, with an investment portfolio of about $1.2 million, and his investment income normally puts him in the top marginal tax bracket.

His estate could be subject to a fair amount of probate taxes. What he needs is a strategy that will minimize taxes and other expenses upon death while still achieving his retirement and estate planning goals.

One solution would be to incorporate a holding company. He could then transfer the investment portfolio in return for shares and debt. This could be done on a "rollover" basis. He would not trigger any of the gains on the investments at that time and no tax would be payable. The company would take over the investments at his tax cost.

Benefits galore

What are the benefits of incorporating a holding company? For one, the man can have a separate will that gifts the shares to his children, thus avoiding probate fees.

There are other benefits, as well. He can pay himself dividends or redeem shares to provide for his living expenses, as well as paying himself a director's fee. This fee represents earned income that creates room for an RRSP contribution. He can even make an over-contribution to his RRSP the year he turns 69. This amount can be deducted in the following year even though his RRSP has been matured into an RRIF or annuity. And, he can also enact an "estate freeze" to pass on future growth in the value of the company to his children.

Paying the price

Obviously, setting up a holding company has merit, but it doesn't come without baggage. There are set-up costs for the company, and the ongoing legal and accounting requirements must also be considered.

Also, the children are going to get shares instead of specific assets. This means that they will have to agree on corporate actions in dealing with the underlying assets. Depending on the type of investments, you may also have transfer and regis-tration costs.

In addition, there is the potential for double taxation in the future. When the individual dies and passes the shares to his children, this will trigger capital gains on the increase in value of his shares in the company. Then, when the company dispos-es of the investments, this will also trigger capital gains. Given these other issues, you must be sure that the tax benefits justify the use of this planning technique.

IN THE NEXT CHAPTER

- Getting older is not getting easier
- Retirement is now more complicated
- Taking stock of finances and requirements
- What to expect from the government
- Creating financial independence
- The details of retirement and pensions
- Making the most of your RRSP
- Real estate considerations
- Your other assets
- All about annuities

5

It's a lot of hard work to retire right

Planning your retirement is a serious business

IF I HAD KNOWN HOW OLD I WAS
GOING TO BE I'D HAVE TAKEN
BETTER CARE OF MYSELF.
—Adolph Zukor

You don't have to be approaching your 100th birthday to relate to Adolph Zukor's sentiment. We could all do a little better in preparing for our retirement years, which by all counts will soon exceed the duration of our working years thanks to breakthroughs in biological and health-care research.

Then how come we don't? For the most part, many people are just too busy dealing with the stresses of day-to-day life to spend much time contemplating arrangements for their retirement and eventual launch into eternity. It's a pity, because most of us recognize that it is something we should do. So there it sits in the back of our minds, just adding to the stress load. Serious stuff.

And that's just it. You have to commit to looking at your present circumstances and plot some future scenarios that you can live with. That's the first, and probably most important, step. Then, you have to spend a little time with a trusted planner. That's all it takes. Once this is taken care of, you'll be surprised how much less stress you have.

You may be wondering why we're talking about retirement in a book about estate planning. Well, the decisions you make today and in your later years regarding how you accumulate and spend your financial assets will have a significant impact on the size and makeup of your estate. It is important for you to have an effective retirement plan that will ensure that there are enough of your assets left over to make the gifts you want to make under your will.

Getting older now takes longer

Thirty years ago, insurance actuaries figured that the average Canadian man was lucky if he reached the ripe old age of 72. What that meant is that most men didn't really require a huge amount of retirement savings because most would expire within seven years of leaving their job.

Women could anticipate living several years longer, but even then a modest retirement arrangement would accommodate their final years. That's all changed now. We've become a nation with superior longevity and there's every indication that this trend will continue.

Not that long ago, people in their forties and fifties were considered ancient. These days, even those in their sixties and seventies are proving that age is just a state of mind. Many could be looking at 20 or 30 more years of active living. And that will require substantially more resources to finance even a modest standard of retirement living.

Not your average retirement

Retirement in Canada has become a complex topic over the past decade. Much of this has to do with Canadians living longer, and requiring lengthier and more expensive health care. And let's not forget the variety of products now available to help us finance the golden years. Retirement planning is a lot like financial planning. You have to understand both your current situation and what you would like to do in retirement before you can start initiating solutions.

The first in-depth examination should involve your current budget—an outline of how your income is being spent. Then, you have to review your budget and determine which expenses will diminish during retirement and which will increase. Typically, by retirement, many people have paid off the mortgage, helped finance their children's education, and invested money on a monthly basis to defray retirement expenses.

Many people feel they will need 70 to 80 percent of their pre-retirement income during retirement to maintain the lifestyle to which they've grown accustomed. While this is generally a good approximation, you really need to document your own retirement needs in detail. Depending on what you want to do, the required income could be significantly higher or lower than the 70 to 80 percent figure. If you plan to travel, buy a condo down south, or even help a grandchild with education costs, your expenses may echo your pre-retirement outlays. Remember that you will also likely lose the benefit of employer paid health coverage. That means you will need to purchase private health insurance, or set aside contingency funds for this purpose.

In addition, you will need to factor in the potential impact of inflation. Although current inflation rates are at manageable levels, this can change. Furthermore, the cost of medical care and prescription drugs may grow at a faster rate than normal inflation, particularly if the various levels of government keep reducing their funding for these types of programs.

Where does it all go?

To help you determine where all that hard-earned income is going, use this form to determine your current spending patterns and project them into retirement.

Living Expenses	Estimated Monthly	Estimated Annually	Estimated into Retirement
Mortgage/Rent			
Property Taxes			
Utilities			
Telephone			
Home Insurance			
Groceries			
Clothing			
Health & Dental Care			
Car Maintenance			
Insurance			
Gas			
Public Transportation			
Entertainment			
Subscriptions			
Cable TV			
Club Fees/Memberships			
Other			
TOTAL ESTIMATED LIVING EXPENSES			

Debt Payments	*Estimated Monthly*	*Estimated Annually*	*Estimated into Retirement*
Car Loan			
Credit Card			
Line of Credit			
Personal Loan			
Other			
TOTAL ESTIMATED DEBT PAYMENTS			
Investment Payments			
Life and Disability Insurance			
RRSP Contributions			
(before Age 69)			
Emergency Fund			
Other Investment Savings			
TOTAL ESTIMATED INVESTMENT PAYMENTS			
Extraordinary Costs			
Gifts			
Vacations			
Charitable Donations			
Other			
TOTAL ESTIMATED EXTRAORDINARY COSTS			
GRAND TOTAL RETIREMENT EXPENSES			

Once you have figured out these expenses, you will begin to get a complete picture of your retirement income needs. Then, you will have to determine if you have the necessary savings—include the growth potential of your investments—to maintain your desired lifestyle during retirement.

Take a look at your RRSPs, your pension plans, and any non-registered assets such as term deposits, stocks, and mutual funds. Then assess your less liquid assets, such as a home, an interest in a business, or things that you might consider selling to create additional retirement capital.

Don't count on a social safety net

While many seniors can rely on Canada Pension Plan (CPP) and Old Age Security (OAS) payments from the federal government, most middle-class–middle-age Canadians should not figure them into their retirement income plans.

There's been a lot of talk over the past few years about whether the CPP will be sustainable as millions of baby boomers turn Canada's demographic pattern on its head. Even if the CPP is around 20 years from now, the chances are good that this program will be limited to lower-income individuals. The same goes for OAS benefits. Even now, benefits under this program are gradually "clawed back" from retirees who have modest income from other sources. Expect nothing and you won't be disappointed.

Try to organize your retirement plan to exclude any government help. In other words, plan to be financially independent. No matter what age you may be now, there are an amazing number of financial products that can help accumulate retirement income and ensure the continued growth of your capital.

If this assumption about government retirement benefits turns out to be wrong, anything you receive from the social safety net will go towards enhancing your standard of living in your retirement years.

Creating your own safety net

Once an analysis of your retirement income requirements is completed, you may find there is insufficient income to meet anticipated needs. In this situation, there are four options to consider. These are not mutually exclusive, and can be mixed and matched.

The best strategy would be to look for ways to free up more investment dollars now. This may mean

- reducing current expenses (i.e., not buying that new car every two or three years);
- looking at ways to reduce your overall tax burden;
- borrowing funds to make new investments (i.e., taking out an investment loan by leveraging some of the equity in your home).

If none of these strategies is available to you, then your next option is to look at ways to reduce expenses on retirement. This could include

- moving to a less expensive home;
- cutting back on travel;
- reducing entertainment expenses;
- being content with one car where you previously had two or more.

A third strategy would be to increase the rate of return on current investments. Translation: a more aggressive investment approach. This will likely require riskier investing, which could backfire if the market goes down before you retire. But for individuals at least 10 to 15 years away from retirement, blue-chip stocks and quality mutual funds are good vehicles for making money work harder. With that kind of timeline, you should easily be able to ride out the normal ups and downs that come with equity investing.

Even retired individuals and those close to retirement may need some growth component in their portfolios. If these individuals rely completely on interest-bearing investments, they could run out of money before the final curtain.

The final and probably least acceptable option is to postpone your plans for retirement. Sadly, this will be the scenario for many Canadians. A large portion of the baby boom generation has not yet amassed the capital or enacted the proper investment strategy to provide for 20 or 30 years of retirement living.

Those of you who are expecting a large inheritance from your parents to see you through should think again. Many of your mothers and fathers are also living longer and using that money for everything from travel to long-term geriatric care.

Don't give up on the RRSP

One of the most important ways to ensure the integrity of your retirement planning is to keep your money in registered plans for as long as possible. Since you must convert an RRSP into income—either a registered annuity or a Registered Retirement Income Fund—at the end of the year in which you turn 69, it is usually in your financial interests to keep your funds in your RRSP until that time to maximize the available tax deferral.

If, at age 65, you have about $250,000 in an RRSP earning 8 percent annually, this will grow to about $340,000 in four years. If you had the same amount in non-registered funds during that same four-year period, it would only grow to about $290,000 on an after-tax basis. That extra $50,000 will provide additional retirement income, which is something we all want in our later years. It is important for you and your adviser to figure out the most effective way to draw against those funds during retirement in order to minimize taxes.

Whether you are withdrawing funds from an RRSP annuity or RRIF, you should ensure that your investments are structured so that your capital is not depleted before your death. If this is done right, you'll have sufficient funds to live well to the end and maybe enough left over to leave your family a little something to remember you by.

Take it now, pay for it later

Buy now and pay later may be a reasonable approach when buying a new fridge or sofa, but when it comes to retirement planning, avoid dipping into various income streams too early.

If you retire early, you have the option to start taking a pension from the Canada Pension Plan at age 60. However, there are fairly substantial penalties in the form of reduced benefits. The same holds true for employer-sponsored registered pension plans. Benefits are significantly reduced if you draw against them before the retirement date set out in the plan.

By drawing upon non-registered investments and avoiding the use of these other programs for just a few years, you will realize a much better standard of living when you eventually start receiving payments at the full amount.

Putting in your 25 years

At one time, company pension plans were the main source of income for most retired workers. Those were the days when it was common for people to stay with the same company for 25 or 30 years. In the past few decades, the workforce has become much more mobile. Many people are moving from employer to employer in search of better opportunities and challenges—and not sticking around long enough to make the company pension plan worthwhile. There is another group of employees that have gone through downsizing or rightsizing and have started their own businesses. As such, more and more people have come to rely on their personal RRSP to fund their retirement.

Still, there are many individuals who belong to a company pension plan, or Registered Pension Plan (RPP). RPPs are governed by the federal Income Tax Act. They are also subject to federal or provincial pension legislation.

The Income Tax Act specifies
- how much can be contributed by the employer and employee to an RPP on a tax-deferred basis;
- the type of investments that the plan can make;
- the tax consequences arising from the payment of benefits under the plan.

Pension legislation specifies
- the terms and conditions of membership in the plan;
- reporting and administrative requirements;
- when benefits can start;
- the type of income options available to retired or departing members.

Pension legislation is not totally uniform across Canada. Even though you may reside in one province, your plan will be governed by the legislation of the province where the company is registered or incorporated.

Details, details, and more details

Individuals who have a Registered Pension Plan at work will belong either to a defined benefit plan or a defined contribution plan.

A defined benefit plan specifies the amount of retirement income provided to the employee based on a formula that normally relates to the individual's length of service and final earnings.

A defined contribution plan will specify the amount of contributions to be made into the plan by the employer and employee. This type of plan resembles an RRSP. The pension benefit is based on the total accumulated value of the contributions and the earnings on those contributions over time. Also, unlike a defined benefit plan, the employee often has several different investment choices.

Although it varies by province, almost all RPPs have restrictions on an employee's ability to access funds in the plan. This is mandated by pension legislation, and these "locking-in" restrictions are designed to ensure that funds are only available for retirement purposes.

If an employee leaves the company before retirement, his or her options are usually restricted to leaving the benefits to accrue in the plan, or transferring the vested contributions into a locked-in RRSP, a Life Income Fund (LIF), certain qualifying annuities, or another RPP.

Rules, rules, and more rules

Cashing out of a plan or transferring the funds into a regular RRSP or RRIF is only permitted in very limited circumstances. For example, a plan member may be entitled to withdraw additional voluntary contributions that he or she made.

Most provinces require the employer to fund at least 50 percent of the benefits accruing after 1986. To the extent that the employee has made contributions that fund benefits in excess of 50 percent of the total, he or she is entitled to a cash refund. In addition, certain provinces such us Ontario and Quebec will provide limited access to RPP funds where the individual can demonstrate "financial hardship."

If you are a member of a defined benefit plan and eligible for early retirement, you may not be able to transfer the commuted value of an RPP to a locked-in RRSP upon termination or retirement. Unless the plan specifically gives the right to transfer benefits, you will have to leave your benefits in the plan and take a pension under the RPP. This removes a significant amount of choice in respect to planning your retirement income.

You should be able to take a life annuity with or without a guaranteed number of payments in the event of early death. The longer the guarantee period, the less income that will be paid under the annuity.

If you are married at the time of retirement, a joint survivor annuity that provides a minimum pension benefit to the surviving spouse must be selected. However, most provinces permit a spouse to waive the requirement for a joint annuity. This would increase the amount of income payable, but it also means the surviving spouse is putting his or her retirement income at risk if the other spouse dies early in retirement. I'll touch on a strategy to deal with this later on in this chapter (see page 70).

Options, options, and more options

An option that most provinces do allow is to transfer the pension funds to a Life Income Fund. This will permit you to direct the investments of the fund in a fashion similar to an RRIF.

If you happen to be married, your spouse must consent to the purchase of a LIF. There are limits placed on the minimum and maximum withdrawals from a LIF, with the minimum payout being the same amount as is required for Registered Retirement Income Funds.

While the maximum payout formula varies from province to province, it is generally designed to ensure that funds are still available when you reach your 80th birthday. At that time, the remaining funds must be used to purchase a lifetime annuity income.

In Alberta, Ontario, and Saskatchewan, it is possible to purchase a Locked-in Retirement Income Fund (LRIF) under pension plans registered in those provinces. Similar to an LIF, an LRIF establishes the minimum and maximum benefit payments. But unlike an LIF, an LRIF does not require you to convert to an annuity at age 80. Quebec recently removed the age limit for LIFs, and it is likely the trend will continue to make LIFs even more flexible.

One more option

There is another option to consider—transferring the commuted value of the pension benefits into a Locked-in Retirement Account (LIRA) or a locked-in RRSP. You can exercise the LIRA approach when you do not want to immediately receive retirement income. This type of plan resembles an RRSP and can invest in similar ways.

However, funds in this type of plan cannot be cashed in or converted, and certain forms of survivor benefits must be provided. When you want to access the funds, they must be used to purchase a qualifying annuity or a Life Income Fund.

Just like an RRSP, a LIRA has to be converted to income by the end of the year in which you turn 69. It is subject to the applicable provincial pension legislation, and you can designate a beneficiary under the plan. This allows the proceeds to flow outside the estate when the plan owner passes on, which helps to avoid probate and other expenses. And just like with a regular RRSP, you are allowed a tax-sheltered rollover where the surviving spouse is the designated beneficiary and transfers this amount into his or her own RRSP.

When you run out of options

You may be wondering what happens if you die while a member of the Registered Pension Plan. If death occurs before retirement, the plan will normally pay a death benefit. The amount will depend on provincial legislation, as well as the terms and type of pension plan.

For a defined benefit plan, benefits will generally be based on one payment or a combination of two payments. One type of payment will represent your accumulated contributions plus accumulated income. The second type of payment is based on the commuted value of the vested pension benefits.

If the deceased is a member of a defined contribution plan, the benefits are normally the value of all vested contributions plus accumulated income.

If your spouse is the recipient of the death benefit, it can be rolled over to another RPP, RRSP, or RRIF to avoid current taxation. Under present rules, if there is no spouse and the benefit is paid to a dependent child or grandchild, the funds can be used to purchase a payout annuity to age 18 to defer tax over a period of time. Recent legislation transfers the tax bill to a financially dependent child even if there is a surviving spouse.

If retirement benefits have commenced and the plan owner dies, several things can happen. If the plan member chose a single life annuity, payments will only continue until the expiry of the guaranteed term. Typically, a guaranteed term of 10 years is selected.

Under a joint survivor annuity, the surviving spouse will receive a reduced pension for the rest of his or her life and will pay tax as the amounts are received. Again, a guaranteed term of 10 years is usually selected.

If the funds were transferred to an LIF, any remaining funds will be distributed to the surviving spouse. If there is no surviving spouse, the benefits can be paid to another beneficiary, who will pay tax. As is the case with pre-retirement benefits, the spouse or dependent children can take advantage of certain transfers to other registered plans to defer the payment of tax on the LIF benefit.

Maximizing your many options

For members of defined benefit pension plans, there is a planning strategy designed to increase the amount of retirement income payable. It is commonly referred to as pension maximization and can be used when you want to purchase an annuity with pension funds.

This option is not as popular as it used to be thanks to lower annuity rates and the increased flexibility associated with LIFs. However, many people still select an annuity to provide retirement benefits. It provides a guaranteed return and eliminates the need to manage the investments.

As I mentioned earlier in this chapter, if you are married upon retirement, you must take a joint annuity unless your spouse waives his or her entitlement. This is a very big decision. Adding a spouse as an annuitant could significantly reduce the retirement income payable. And if your spouse predeceases you, this reduction will have served no purpose.

On the other hand, if your spouse waives his or her entitlement to a joint annuity, it could result in significant financial hardship if you die prematurely. This is where life insurance can come to the rescue.

If you own life insurance, or are healthy and can qualify, it might make sense to elect a single life annuity and use the insurance to replace income upon death. In addition to ensuring higher retirement income, the surviving spouse will receive a tax-free death benefit instead of taxable pension benefits.

When choosing between various income options under a pension plan, life insurance provides more flexibility. But be careful. One of the problems with this strategy is that the insurance costs may exceed the increase in income. However, if your insurance is already in force, it will likely be less costly to keep than to switch to the joint annuity option.

Does this work with RRSPs?

It is possible to use a similar strategy in determining the payout option under an RRSP. However, Canada Customs and Revenue Agency has expressed concern with these types of arrangements. Some insurance companies were agreeing to issue insurance policies to uninsurable people, provided that person also purchased a registered life annuity without any guarantee period.

With this arrangement, the insurance company was insulated from the risk of premature death, since the annuity payments would end at that time. Meanwhile, the individual would benefit from a higher income during retirement, and his or her estate would receive a tax-free insurance benefit instead of taxable RRSP proceeds. As a result, CCRA has indicated that it may treat insurance proceeds as a taxable RRSP distribution in arrangements like this.

Nevertheless, you can set up these types of arrangements to minimize any tax issues. First, you have to apply for the life insurance policy. Once the insurer indicates that the policy will be issued on a standard basis, you can arrange for the purchase of a registered annuity with a different insurance company. This should eliminate concerns that CCRA may attempt to link the insurance policy and the registered annuity. And since most Canadians now select RRIFs over annuities, this concept has a much more limited market.

Working your RRSP

Maturity options for RRSPs are more flexible than for RPPs. For example, RRSP funds can be withdrawn in cash at any time, subject to surrender charges or other contractual provisions. The downside is that you immediately trigger tax on the amount withdrawn.

A second option is to use RRSP funds to purchase certain types of annuities. The annuity can be payable for life, with or without a guaranteed minimum number of payments in the event of early death. You can also select a term-certain annuity to age 90, or exercise a "joint and last survivor annuity," where payments continue as long as one spouse is alive.

Unlike annuities under an RPP, a spouse's consent is not needed to elect a single life annuity. Under this kind of annuity, the amount of income payable is based on the size of the deposit, the expected duration of payments, and current interest rates. The younger you are, for example, the lower the payments will be. (The insurance company's expectation is that more payments will have to be made.)

Similarly, lower interest rates mean lower payments. Just as with RPPs, a joint annuity will provide less income than a single life annuity.

Why would someone choose an annuity versus a Registered Retirement Income Fund as a maturity option? An annuity can offer several advantages.

- In a high interest rate environment, you lock in interest rates over your lifetime.
- An annuity is attractive if you want to avoid investment risk and the need to actively manage your retirement funds.
- An annuity guarantees that payments will continue for the selected period of time.
- Annuities are attractive if you are risk-averse and don't have a great deal of investment expertise.

As with just about everything in financial and retirement planning, this is not an all-or-nothing situation. For instance, you can transfer some of your RRSP funds into an annuity and put the remainder into an RRIF.

The big RRIF conversion

Due to their flexibility and investment selection, Registered Retirement Income Funds have become the most popular payout option. As discussed earlier, once you hit the end of the year in which you turn 69, you must do something with your RRSP.

Very few people just cash out—too much of a tax loss. Most choose the RRIF conversion route. Nothing spectacular, just a direct rollover and a few papers to sign, authorizing the transfer of the funds from your RRSPs.

Subject to certain limitations, an RRIF provides you with a high degree of choice regarding where the funds are invested. You may select from guaranteed investment accounts or a variety of equities and bond investments.

And just like your old RRSP, your RRIF is subject to some basic rules. Any income earned on RRIF investments continues to be tax sheltered. You are, however, still subject to the foreign investment limits—25 percent maximum for 2000 and up to 30 percent for the tax year 2001.

Money only goes one way in an RRIF

Of course, you can't keep contributing to an RRIF, and you do have to withdraw a certain percentage of the fund's capital every year. This amount is based on your age and fund value at the beginning of each year, and the percentage increases each year. Even if you only withdraw the minimum each year, the fund value will start to decline once the minimum percentage withdrawal exceeds the investment income being earned. It is possible to base the income payments on the age of your spouse. Assuming your spouse is younger than you, this will reduce the required withdrawal from the RRIF.

There are no restrictions on maximum withdrawals, so it is possible to withdraw all the funds from an RRIF. While this flexibility is very handy, it could also lead to a situation where you expend your retirement income long before you take your last breath!

RRIFs also allow you to convert all or a portion of its funds into an annuity in the future. This might be a good idea if interest rates increase in the future or you want to shift the investment responsibility to your insurance company.

What else have you got?

When you look at Canadian financial portfolios, most people still have more money tied up in investments other than their RRSPs. Remember that only about a third of all Canadians make an annual contribution to an RRSP in any given year, and only 10 percent of those maximize that contribution.

Where do these people keep their financial worth? Much of it is in their house—actually, it is their house. In the 1970s and 1980s, that was not a bad plan. High demand for housing coupled with rampant inflation saw housing values soar in many parts of the country. However, with higher interest rates and the recession in the early 1990s, real estate prices headed south.

We've had a bit of a resurgent market since the end of that recession, and the housing market has rolled along nicely into the new century. But we cannot expect the market to deliver the kind of growth it did 15 to 20 years ago.

Individuals who are now heading towards retirement, and especially those now retired, should take a good look at their housing status. With the departure of their children, this could be the time to downsize to a more manageable property, especially in terms of upkeep. Downsizing could also free up some of the equity acquired in the last two decades or more.

For some individuals, a larger sum of capital for investment can be had by selling their home outright, investing the proceeds, and renting a condo.

Backing out of the house

Some people are drawn to yet another option—the reverse mortgage. A reverse mortgage allows individuals who have mortgage-free homes to convert their equity into retirement income.

Usually, a financial institution will advance between 40 to 60 percent of the home's value to you and then take back a mortgage on the home. Typically, you use the loaned funds to purchase an annuity to supplement other sources of retirement income. No principal or interest has to be paid until the home is sold or you expire. This gives you full access to the loaned funds while you are alive.

The interesting part is what happens if you live a lot longer than you or the bank ever expected, and the loan and accumulated interest threaten to exceed the value of the house at the current market value. Not to worry, the financial institutions involved are quite aware of this possibility, and agree to not call the loan while the individual is alive and continues to own the house. Also, the loans are structured on a 'limited recourse' basis so that the lender can only rely on the proceeds of sale from the home to satisfy the outstanding debt. The lender cannot sue the individual or his or her estate if the loan exceeds the proceeds of sale. The lender assumes this risk. As a result, interest charged on the loan is usually higher than on a regular residential mortgage to take into account this increased risk. Also, as already noted, the lender will usually only lend a maximum of 60% of the current value of the home.

This can work to your advantage when dealing with the tax issue involved with an annuity purchased through a reverse mortgage. A portion of each annuity payment consists of taxable income. However, the interest expense—and remember it's higher than on a regular mortgage—creates an offsetting deduction against the income. In most situations, then, there is no net taxable income, or it only represents a small portion of the total payments.

Don't throw caution to the wind

Like many strategies that sound practical, there are some drawbacks to a reverse mortgage. The main problem is that it can significantly reduce the value of your estate. The compounding interest on the loan will rapidly erode your equity in the property. This is of particular concern where the value of the home is not growing or is in fact decreasing. In most cases, the main impact is felt by the heirs to your estate, but you can directly bear this cost if the house has to be sold prior to your death.

The bottom line? Reverse mortgages do allow seniors to continue living in their own homes while creating another source of retirement income. But these arrangements can have a very negative impact on the individual's net worth over time.

For these reasons, there is only limited use of reverse mortgages in Canada. They may be a very good option in certain situations, perhaps where other options aren't available. Reverse mortgages are also an option for individuals who have a less than amiable relationship with their children.

The rest of your stuff

Do you own your own home, and have a tidy and expanding sum tucked in an RRSP? Compared to most Canadians, you're doing pretty well. If you have all of this and some non-registered investments outside of that RRSP, you are either close to becoming, or have already become, a charter member of the financially independent. Just make sure those non-registered term deposits, mutual and segregated funds, and stocks are tended to properly. Don't try this at home without professional investment advice. Work with your adviser to select investments that match your risk and investment profile while maximizing the after-tax rate of return.

If you have a decade or two to ramble through before you hit retirement, then taking on a bit more risk—including more equities in your portfolio—is a sensible approach. You want your assets to deliver solid gains, and you have time on your side to weather any roller-coaster action on the Canadian and international stock markets.

If you are nearing retirement, you need a more balanced approach, and you will need to have greater liquidity—assets that are readily converted to cash. Your investments should provide you with finances to meet two demands—ensuring a guaranteed level of income to meet retirement needs and protecting your income from the effects of inflation.

One strategy is to place sufficient assets in relatively risk-free investments to cover your projected retirement income needs. Any additional capital can be invested in more volatile investments with a view to achieving a superior rate of return. Since this capital will not be required immediately, it will have time to compound and ride out market fluctuations. If you have 15 to 25 years of retirement living to finance, this growth component is vital.

Divide and conquer

Military strategists have always realized that if you split your enemy into various camps you have a better chance of cleaning their clocks. Surprisingly, this approach can also work well within your investment portfolio. By splitting your assets up and sending them off in different directions, you can usually make some great financial strides. It's called diversification.

Because older investors require a more balanced portfolio, diversification is even more important for them than for younger investors. This approach protects against the significant losses that can arise from being overweighted in any one type of investment.

Retired individuals typically have less time to recover from a market loss. They must take steps to protect themselves, and diversification can do just that. This means diversification between investment types, sector representation in equity investments, and geographic regions. For example, it may make sense to use non-registered investments to purchase mutual funds whose performance is based on the U.S., European, or other global markets. This will offset the foreign content restrictions for pension and RRSP investments.

Retirees may also want more guaranteed-type investments in their RRSPs, with dividend and capital growth investments slated for non-registered investments. This will allow for the diversification of the entire portfolio, while the retirees take advantage of the preferential tax treatment available to dividend income and capital gains.

Enter the annuity factor

There is another investment vehicle that can provide guaranteed income as well as preferential tax treatment. Prescribed annuities are non-registered immediate annuities that meet certain conditions set out in the Income Tax Act. These rules govern who is entitled to own and receive payments under the contract. Corporations and certain trusts cannot. The regulations also specify the type and duration of payments that can be made.

As noted, a prescribed annuity is purchased with non-registered funds. An immediate or payout annuity converts the lump sum deposit into a stream of income over a term of years selected by the investor. This type of product is often used during retirement.

It is important to know that you can designate a beneficiary under both a deferred and immediate annuity. If your spouse or children are named, the policy may be protected from your creditors as well as creditors of your estate. This makes annuity products attractive to professionals and business owners who are concerned about personal liability.

Another bonus is that if you name a beneficiary, upon death any remaining value will flow outside of your estate, avoiding probate fees and other expenses.

Payments under the annuity represent a return of the original deposit plus interest income, and the tax treatment of these products certainly add to their appeal. Unlike a regular annuity, the original capital is treated as being returned on an equal basis over the payment period. This means that the initial payments are subject to less tax than a regular annuity, providing an element of tax deferral.

Softening the tax bite

A theoretical case might help to clarify this. Let's consider Fred, a 67-year-old with $100,000 in Canada Savings Bonds. Fred plans to use the interest to supplement his other retirement income. If necessary, he might dip into the capital to pay for extraordinary expenses.

Assuming he is in a 40 percent tax bracket and could earn 5 percent on the CSBs, he would retain $3,000 of interest annually after-tax. Alternatively, he could cash in the CSBs and purchase a prescribed annuity contract through an insurance company. The insurance company will pay him an income over his lifetime or for a specified number of years. The amount of this income will depend on the size of the deposit, the guaranteed interest rate, and the duration of the payments.

Suppose Fred purchases a life annuity that pays him $8,400 per year. The tax rules assume that the original deposit of $100,000 will be paid back in equal instalments based on the expected number of payments. Where the annuity payments continue over the lifetime of an annuitant, there is a prescribed mortality table to determine the expected number of payments. For a 67-year-old male, the expected number of payments is 17 years. So, of the $8,400 annual payment to Fred, $5,900 will be considered a return of the original deposit ($100,000 divided by 17 years). The remaining $2,500 is treated as interest income.

This provides Fred with $7,400 ($8,400 minus 40 percent of $2,500) each year on an after-tax basis—considerably higher than the $3,000 from the CSBs. The higher income is partly the result of the original capital being returned to him and partly the result of tax deferral, since in the early years less interest income is reported and there is less tax to pay.

Also, because a prescribed annuity is a long-term investment, the deposits will normally earn a higher rate of return than CSBs or term deposits. A win-win proposition.

There is one more thing to consider. If Fred continued to own the CSBs, he would still have $100,000 when he died, which could go to his beneficiaries. Under a prescribed annuity, he uses up all his capital and has nothing to pass on to his family. If he is insurable, all is not lost. Fred could purchase insurance to replace all or some of the original capital upon his death. For example, the cost for $100,000 of Term to 100 life insurance would be $3,600 per year. The following tells the tale:

Income from Prescribed Annuity	$8,400
Tax on Taxable Portion	$1,000 ($2,500 x 40 percent)
Net Income (After-Tax)	$7,400
Insurance Costs for $100,000 of Term to 100	$3,600
Total Income	$3,800

Even after factoring in insurance costs, Fred will have more income on an after-tax basis than if he had just hung on to his CSBs. Plus, by naming a beneficiary under the life insurance policy, the proceeds will be paid directly to the beneficiary, avoiding probate fees and expenses, as well as estate creditors.

For the right individual, this can be a very attractive strategy. But he or she

- has to recognize that the arrangement is not flexible once in place—the original capital is fully committed to the annuity and life insurance premiums;
- needs to have other liquid funds available to help out with unanticipated expenses;
- has to understand that the interest rate is locked in and will not change in the future—this can be an advantage if interest rates fall and a disadvantage if interest rates rise.

IN THE NEXT CHAPTER

- Protect yourself from excess taxation
- Transferring property
- Protecting your RRSP or RRIF
- More about trusts
- Out-of-country tax issues
- Owning property in the U.S.

6

Closing the vault

The taxman can and will
follow you to the grave

IT'S NOT THAT I'M AFRAID OF
DEATH, I JUST DON'T WANT TO
BE THERE WHEN IT HAPPENS.
—Woody Allen

Just like Woody Allen, most of us are squeamish about
what's waiting for us towards the back end of this existence.
On the plus side, Allen also noted that at least death is one
of the few things that can be done just as easily lying down.

Despite the uncertainties surrounding death, there's one thing
you can count on at the end—the tax department wanting to get
a piece of the action. This is one thing that you should not take
lying down. You may not be able to avoid paying some tax, but
there are some planning ideas you can employ to minimize taxes
upon death, and even after.

Don't let your heirs get cut

As you may recall, passing property upon death to the surviving
spouse or a spousal trust will not trigger a tax liability for the
deceased's estate. A spousal trust entitles the deceased's spouse
to all of the trust income. As long as the spouse is alive, he or she
will be the only person entitled to capital distribution. When
property is transferred to a spouse or spousal trust, there will be

a deferral of tax on capital gains until the spouse disposes of the property or dies.

Why would you set up a spousal trust instead of giving it directly to your spouse? There are a couple of reasons. A spousal trust is commonly used when the person making the will has remarried, and there are children from the first marriage. If you leave your property to your second spouse, and he or she remarries, your children from the first marriage may not receive anything when your second spouse dies. A spousal trust ensures that the surviving spouse is taken care of, while still controlling how the property is distributed upon his or her death.

Post-mortem control

If you have concerns about your spouse's ability to deal with the property in the estate, you may also want to use a spousal trust. If the main assets of your estate are shares in a private corporation, for example, and your spouse has not been actively involved in its operations, it might be wise to lay out some guiding principles.

While you may want the business to remain in the family, you might not want to burden your spouse with the management. You could set up a spousal trust and appoint a business associate and/or other family members to act as co-trustees.

There may be situations where you want to leave property to your spouse or spousal trust but still realize all or a portion of any capital gains. For example, you may have access to the $500,000 capital gains exemption for shares in small businesses or qualifying farm property. Or, there may be a capital loss carry forward or charitable donations that could be used to offset capital gains in the year of death. The Income Tax Act allows your estate and spouse to elect out of the spousal rollover on certain properties in order to trigger a taxable gain or deductible loss.

This way, your capital gains exemption or allowable capital losses can offset any gain. And your surviving spouse then inherits the property with a higher cost base, resulting in less tax to pay when he or she disposes of the property.

Taking it a step further

You can also reduce taxes if you want to make gifts to both your spouse and other family members. This involves specifying in your will that your spouse is to receive property with appreciated gains or providing your executor with some discretion on how to distribute the assets of the estate.

For example, assume your estate consists of assets with unrealized capital gains, and other assets such as term deposits and bank accounts. To minimize taxes, your executor could satisfy a bequest to your spouse through the transfer of the property with unrealized capital gains. The term deposits and cash, which have no capital gains liability, could then be transferred to the other family members. This way, you avoid the realization of the capital gains that would otherwise result if those assets were transferred to a non-spousal beneficiary.

The executor will pick and choose between your estate's assets in satisfying the bequests under the will. The goal will be to try and satisfy the spouse's share with appreciated assets.

RRSPs and RRIFs can be fair game

As mentioned earlier, the full value of your RRSP or RRIF is taxable upon death. This can trigger a significant tax liability to the estate. But as you may remember, that tax can be avoided if your surviving spouse is designated as the plan's beneficiary.

If you designate financially dependent children as beneficiaries, they will be responsible for the tax bill on your RRSP or RRIF. This can work to the family's advantage if the children are in a lower tax bracket. As well, dependent children under the age of 18 can spread out this tax bill through the purchase of an annuity for a term up to their 18th birthday.

If a child is dependent by reason of mental or physical infirmity, he or she can transfer the full amount received to his or her RRSP. This provides for a much longer period of tax deferral than normal.

So, in determining who is to receive the value of your RRSP or RRIF upon death, consider the tax advantages of designating your spouse or financially dependent children as beneficiaries.

The gift that still keeps giving

There is another point about RRSPs that is often overlooked. When an individual dies, the executor cannot contribute to the deceased's RRSP, even if that person had unused contribution room in the year of death.

Does this mean that the RRSP deduction is lost? Not necessarily. If the surviving spouse is under the age of 70, the executor of the deceased's estate can make a contribution to his or her RRSP within 60 days after the end of the year of death. This can result in considerable tax savings, particularly if the deceased has substantial unused RRSP contribution room from previous years.

A trustworthy strategy

Another simple way to minimize taxation upon death involves the use of trusts under a will. These are known as testamentary trusts. Trusts will be discussed in more detail in Chapter 8, but I wanted to touch on their tax-reducing potential here.

In your will, you can create a testamentary trust for minor children or for disabled beneficiaries. A trust ensures the safekeeping of the trust assets while the beneficiary is a minor or continues to suffer from some incapacity. The appointed trustee will be responsible for investing the trust assets, and making payments of capital and income to the beneficiaries.

In the case of a testamentary trust for minor children, the trust is normally wound up when the children reach a certain age. At that time, property remaining in the trust is distributed to the children. A testamentary trust established for a disabled beneficiary may continue as long as that beneficiary is alive.

Another advantage is that a testamentary trust is treated as a separate entity, despite what the beneficiary earns from other sources. As a result, it qualifies for the graduated tax rates available to individuals. As a result, trust income under approximately $30,000 qualifies for the lowest marginal tax rate. A testamentary trust can therefore be used to split income with the beneficiaries and reduce the amount of combined taxes paid. The more trusts created under the will, the more potential for income splitting and tax savings.

The one trick is to establish a separate trust for each minor beneficiary—it's much more effective than creating a single trust for all of them. This approach can save tens of thousands of dollars in taxes if the trusts are earning a lot of income and there is a large number of minor children who are beneficiaries.

This strategy also makes sense for beneficiaries who aren't minors. In this case, each adult beneficiary could be one of the trustees of their own trust. This will provide that person with some control over the use of the funds, and disbursement of income and capital.

One word of caution: be aware of the administrative costs and time commitment for maintaining these separate trusts—and the need for competent trustees.

When the Internal Revenue Service comes a-calling

The economic boom that followed World War II and the similar boom that has gripped Canada for the past six or seven years has provided a lot of Canadians with a fairly comfortable living. Many have used this wealth to avoid our harsh winters by purchasing condos or homes in places such as Florida or Arizona.

What many Canadians may not realize is that owning this type of property exposes them to U.S. estate taxes. Here's how these rules work, plus some ideas on how to reduce the potential tax bite. And the Internal Revenue Service (IRS) does bite.

Citizenship is a legal concept and is normally determined by the person's place of birth, or the citizenship of his or her parents. It is possible to be a dual citizen. This could happen if a person's parents are citizens of two different countries, or if a child is born in a different country than his or her parents.

A country's citizen is normally given specific legal rights, including the right to vote, to travel freely within that country, and to work in that country. It is difficult to change your citizenship—usually a person must legally renounce citizenship and apply for citizenship in another country.

While a person's citizenship is not relevant for Canadian tax rules, this is not true for other countries, such as the United States. Citizens of the U.S. remain liable for both U.S. income taxes and estate taxes on their worldwide income, even if they no longer reside in the United States.

Determining a person's residency for tax purposes can get quite involved. The Canadian courts have defined residency as the place where, in the settled routine of life, a person normally or customarily lives.

Since most countries tax individuals based on their residency, there are statutory rules that can also come into play in determining the residency of an individual. For example, the Income Tax Act will deem a person to be a Canadian resident if he or she spends 183 days or more in Canada in any given year. For tax purposes, it is also possible to be a resident in more than one country.

However, most countries have entered into agreements called Tax Treaties. These treaties set out rules to avoid double taxation—including which country has primary taxing jurisdiction if a person is considered by law to be a resident in two countries. The whole thing can be quite complex and is best left for your accounting specialist to assess and make recommendations.

What Uncle Sam wants

If you are a Canadian resident and citizen, you may still be subject to U.S. estate taxes if you own U.S. situs property. "Situs" is a legal term that means owning property located in the United States—like a condo in Arizona, shares of a U.S. corporation, debt obligations issued by U.S. residents, or personal property located in the U.S., such as cars, boats, or home furnishings.

Estate tax is levied on the full value of the U.S. situs assets as evaluated at the date of death. Here's a chart that shows the rate of tax on various estate values.

Base for Tentative Tax		Tentative Tax	
Over (in $)	*But Not Over (in $)*	*This Amount + (in $)*	*This Percent on Excess*
–	10,000	–	18%
10,000	20,000	1,800	20%
20,000	40,000	3,800	22%
40,000	60,000	8,200	24%
60,000	80,000	13,000	26%
80,000	100,000	18,200	28%
100,000	150,000	23,800	30%
150,000	250,000	38,800	32%
250,000	500,000	70,800	34%
500,000	750,000	155,800	37%
750,000	1,000,000	248,300	39%
1,000,000	1,250,000	345,800	41%
1,250,000	1,500,000	448,300	43%
1,500,000	2,000,000	555,800	45%
2,000,000	2,500,000	780,800	49%
2,500,000	3,000,000	1,025,800	53%
3,000,000		1,290,800	55%

For example, let's assume that a Canadian resident owned U.S. situs assets valued at $230,000 on death. According to the chart, the tax on the first $150,000 would be $38,800, and an additional 32% would be levied on the excess of $80,000, for a total U.S. estate tax (before credits) of $64,400.

As you can see, the rates start at 18 percent and reach 55 percent for estates with a value over U.S.$3 million. Fortunately, the Canada-U.S. Tax Treaty contains a number of provisions that will reduce this tax burden for Canadians. One rule provides that if the deceased's total estate is worth less than U.S.$1.2 million, only real estate and certain business assets located in the U.S. will be subject to estate tax.

In addition, Canadians are currently entitled to a credit of up to U.S.$220,550, which can offset tax on up to U.S.$675,000 of taxable estate values. This credit will increase every year to 2006, when it will shelter up to U.S.$1 million in taxable estate values. Here's a table that sets out these credits:

Year	Exclusion Amount (in $)	Applicable Credit (in $)
2000	675,000	220,550
2001	675,000	220,550
2002	700,000	229,800
2003	700,000	229,800
2004	850,000	287,300
2005	950,000	326,300
2006	1,000,000	345,800

Let's look at a hypothetical situation to see how this credit system works. Don is in his sixties. He's a Canadian resident and citizen, and has about $1 million in total assets. Don is planning to purchase a condominium in the U.S. for $200,000. He doesn't have any significant liabilities.

Based on current exchange rates, Don's total estate is worth about U.S.$650,000 and the condo will be worth about U.S.$130,000. The amount of the credit Don's estate could claim against estate taxes is based on the ratio of his U.S. assets to his worldwide assets. In this case, he can claim 20 percent of the total credit of U.S.$220,550—about U.S.$44,000. Based on the table above, this will offset taxes on the first U.S.$165,000 of value. So, at this time, he doesn't have to worry about U.S. estate taxes.

But if his Canadian estate grows in value before his death, to say U.S.$1.3 million, Don will have a problem. In this case, the credit will only be U.S.$22,050, but his estate tax liability will be about U.S.$33,000. This would leave him with a tax bill of about U.S.$11,000, or approximately Cdn.$17,000.

Should have bought in Penticton

As a result of recent changes to the Canada-U.S. Tax Treaty, estate taxes payable by a Canadian resident will be creditable against Canadian taxes in the year of death, to the extent that the Canadian taxes relate to the taxable U.S. assets. For example, if Don's condo increased in value from U.S.$130,000 to U.S.$200,000, there would be a capital gain of U.S.$70,000, or about Cdn.$100,000. This would translate into a tax bill of about Cdn.$25,000 upon death.

Any estate taxes payable in respect to the condo could be claimed as a credit against the $25,000 Canadian tax. But if Don had no Canadian taxes payable in respect to the U.S. assets, there would be no credit available to his estate.

If Don is married, the property can be transferred to his surviving spouse via a rollover for Canadian tax purposes. This will avoid capital gains taxes.

The Canada-U.S. Tax Treaty also provides a marital tax credit, up to the current credit limit, where U.S. situs property is left to the surviving spouse. The amount of this credit is generally the lesser of the prorated credit available to the deceased and the amount of estate taxes otherwise payable on the transferred property. In effect, Don's estate would receive a double tax credit if the condo is transferred to his spouse upon death.

In several respects, then, the Canada-U.S. Tax Treaty has significantly reduced the impact that U.S. estate taxes will have on most Canadians.

Where there is potential exposure to U.S. estate taxes, there are four common planning techniques you can employ.

1. Marital credit

As discussed above, by gifting the taxable U.S. property to your surviving spouse, you can double the tax credit available to your estate. Let's use Don's hypothetical situation again to explain how this works.

Assume that upon death Don's estate is worth U.S.$1.3 million, and the condo continues to be valued at U.S.$130,000. The U.S. estate taxes payable on the condo would be about U.S.$33,000. Don's estate would be entitled to a prorated tax credit of U.S.$22,050 (U.S.$130,000 ÷ U.S.$1.3 million x U.S.$220,500).

If he leaves the condo to his wife, however, not only does Don avoid Canadian tax on the capital gain, but his estate will qualify for the marital tax credit.

The marital credit is the lesser of the U.S.$22,050 credit available to his estate and the U.S.$33,000 estate taxes payable on the condo. With this scenario, Don's estate could claim another credit of U.S.$22,050, eliminating the estate tax liability.

2. Non-recourse debt

This planning technique, using non-recourse loans, takes advantage of how the value of property is determined for estate tax purposes. Let's say from our scenario above that Don plans to borrow U.S.$75,000 to help finance the purchase of his condo. Normally, the financial institution will secure this debt by taking a mortgage against the property. In this case, however, the financial institution retains the right to go against Don personally if the condo's value declines below the amount outstanding under the mortgage. This is known as a full recourse loan. However, if Don gets his financial institution to agree that the security for the loan is limited to the value of the condo, he will have secured a non-recourse loan.

Would a bank be willing to provide non-recourse financing? That depends on how competitive the lending market is at the time. Non-recourse loans are easier to negotiate if the amount of the loan is a small portion of the property's total value, or the borrower agrees to pay a higher rate of interest to compensate the lender for the extra risk.

The reason it is important for Don to obtain non-recourse financing is that his estate would be entitled to deduct the loan directly against the value of the condo in determining the liability for estate taxes.

If the condo is worth U.S.$150,000 at the time of his death, for example, and the outstanding non-recourse mortgage is U.S.$60,000, the property would be valued at U.S.$90,000. Consequently, the taxes would be calculated on that amount.

3. Holding U.S. assets in a Canadian company

If there is the potential for a large estate tax bill, more sophisticated planning may be required—such as incorporating a Canadian company to hold U.S. situs assets, such as stocks, debt certificates, and real estate.

Since shares in Canadian companies are not considered U.S. situs property, holding these shares upon death should not trigger a U.S. estate tax bill. There are, however, a number of considerations in setting up a Canadian company for this purpose, such as:

- the expense of establishing and maintaining a corporation
- if the U.S. assets include recreational property, such as a condominium, the individual risks being taxed in Canada for the personal use of that property

- the U.S. Internal Revenue Service may attempt to "look through" the corporation and treat the assets as if they were owned personally by the shareholder

Before putting a strategy like this into action, expert tax and legal advice should be the order of the day. These types of arrangements can become very complicated.

4. Life insurance

When you consider the implementation costs of some of the above-mentioned solutions, purchasing life insurance may be the most cost-effective method of taking care of the tax bill.

If you are married and plan to leave property to your spouse, you might want to structure the insurance on a joint second-to-die basis. The tax bill upon the first death may not be that significant due to the extra marital deduction and the capital gains rollover under Canadian tax rules. The majority of the taxes will be triggered upon the second death, and that is when the insurance pays out. And keep in mind that this insurance is less expensive because it only pays out upon the second death.

IN THE NEXT CHAPTER
- Charitable giving
- Rules that have changed
- Tying in life insurance
- Giving publicly traded investments
- Gifts of capital property
- Private foundations

7

Keep a charitable thought

It's the thought that counts, and if you want to share the wealth you'll have to do a little thinking

MONEY IS LIKE MANURE.
WHEN YOU PILE IT UP IT STINKS.
WHEN YOU SPREAD IT AROUND,
IT MAKES THINGS GROW.
—Murray Koffler

Charity begins at home. But once things are taken care of there, we tend to extend a helping hand to the rest of the human family on this ever-shrinking planet.

Helping out makes us feel good. Sure, people talk of tax breaks for charitable donations, but for most of us it still boils down to making life more comfortable for those less fortunate than us. That's not to say you shouldn't partake of the tax advantages of giving; certainly the more money you retain, the more money you have to spread around.

It might be useful to review the general tax rules on charitable gifting as they apply while an individual is alive and upon death.

Don't lose those receipts

The first $200 worth of charitable donations qualifies for a federal tax credit of 17 percent. Anything above $200 qualifies for a federal credit equal to 29 percent. This credit can reduce provincial taxes as well as surtaxes, significantly reducing the cost of making the donation in the first place.

It is also possible for married couples to pool their receipts and have one person (usually the one who can use the credit the most) claim the credit.

For example, if a husband and wife each made $200 donations and claimed them in their own returns, the combined federal credit would be $68—$34 for each of their $200 donations. However, if the wife claims all the donations (totalling $400), she would receive total federal credits of $92 (17 percent for the first $200 and 29 percent for the remaining $200). That's an extra $24.

Pooling the donations also makes sense if one spouse has little or no taxable income, since the credit is non-refundable. The person in a tax-paying position should claim the credit to maximize the benefits of the family's donations.

Another important rule to keep in mind is that charitable gifts made through a person's will are deemed to have been made in the year of death. This can be useful in offsetting taxes that arise as a result of death, such as capital gains taxes.

If the gift cannot be fully utilized as a credit in the year of death, it can be carried back to the prior year's tax return and a tax refund may be available.

Rules keep changing

During the deficit years of the early 1990s, the federal and provincial governments cut back spending in all areas, including support of the charitable sector. That lack of financial support continues today. The result is obvious: charities are having a tough time making ends meet. To try and alleviate some of their financial difficulties, charities and their advisers lobbied for changes in the tax rules to provide more incentives for charitable gifting. And, surprise, surprise, there have been a number of enhancements.

They are as follows:

1. New limits

The amount of the gift that would qualify for the tax credit used to be limited to 20 percent of net income in the year of the gift. This could have an impact on the credit claimed, if the size of the gift was large in relation to the individual's net income. For example, if someone made a gift of $40,000 to the Heart and Stroke Foundation, and his or her net income was $60,000 in that year, the maximum amount of the gift he or she could claim in the year would be $12,000.

The rules did allow you to carry forward the excess contribution of $28,000 and claim it against net income for up to five years in the future. But if the individual died prior to claiming all of the credit, the benefit would be lost.

If a donation was made in the year of death (through the will or otherwise), it was also subject to the 20 percent limit. In that situation, if the credit could not be fully utilized in the year of death, the estate could only carry back the excess gift to the prior year's tax return.

There was no opportunity to carry forward the gift and use it against the estate's future tax liabilities. This certainly discouraged large gifts made through a will.

But the new rules have changed the entire landscape. First of all, gifts made before death now have a limit of 75 percent of net income. Perhaps more importantly, the income limit has been increased to 100 percent for gifts made in the year of death, including gifts through the will.

This significantly reduces the likelihood that the charitable credit will not be fully utilized upon death.

Tying in life insurance

Life insurance is often used to establish a large gift upon death. The new rules make this type of gifting much more advantageous for tax purposes.

In the past, the most common approach was to either gift an existing policy to a charity or purchase a new policy and set up the charity as the owner. If an existing policy was used, the cash surrender value of the policy would represent a charitable gift. Because the transfer of the policy would result in its disposition, there was a possibility of a taxable income to the donor if the policy was in a gain position at the time of transfer. If the donor continued to make premium payments under the charity's direction, such payments would be treated as a charitable donation.

The same is true for premiums paid on new policies. While the donor would bear the future cost of the insurance premiums, this cost would be reduced by the tax credit. However, since the charity is now the policy's owner and beneficiary, no tax credit would be available when the death benefit is paid.

In effect, with the charity being the owner and beneficiary of the policy, the premium paid by the donor would represent a charitable gift, but the death benefit would not.

Use it before they lose it

As a point of interest, charities are required to expend on charitable activities 80 percent of all gifts for which they issue receipts in the previous year. With a cash gift, this is not usually a problem. However, if the gift is property, such as an insurance policy, there is no cash available to use on charitable activities. If a charity receives too many gifts of this nature, it may have trouble satisfying these disbursement requirements.

This problem can be avoided if the donor directs that the gift be held for 10 years before it can be used. The Income Tax Act provides that such gifts are not included in the charity's 80% disbursement requirement until the expiry of the 10-year direction. Therefore, for those considering gifting an insurance policy to a charity, it would be helpful to direct that the gift of the premium be held by the designated charity for the required 10-year period. This direction would apply to each premium paid under the policy, as well as any death benefit.

For someone who dies within 10 years of the last premium payment, the death benefit has to be held by the charity until the 10-year period expires. In this situation, it might be prudent to purchase an insurance policy, such as universal life, where the death benefit can be funded over a short period of time. This would give the charity access to the insurance proceeds more quickly in the event of a premature death.

Everyone can benefit

There is another way that a gift of life insurance can be put together. Specifically, the donor purchases and continues to own the policy. Upon the donor's death, the insurance proceeds flow through the estate and out to the charity.

Alternatively, as a result of recent tax changes, the charity can now be designated as the beneficiary of the policy and receive the proceeds directly from the insurance company. By designating the charity as the beneficiary, the insurance proceeds do not flow through the estate, and therefore probate fees and estate creditors are avoided.

In this situation, the donor cannot claim a credit for the insurance premium, but a credit is available in the year of death equal to the insurance proceeds. This credit can help eliminate tax liabilities in the year of death, and any excess credits can be carried back to the prior year's tax return.

Let's consider the following example to get a better idea of how this works. Sheri is recently widowed and is looking at structuring a major gift to a favoured charity upon her passing. She could purchase an insurance policy with a death benefit of $100,000. The premium for a Term to 100 policy would be in the range of $2,400 per year.

If Sheri continued to be the owner of the policy, with her estate designated as beneficiary, this premium would not qualify as a charitable contribution. Her will would gift the death benefit to her favourite charity. Alternatively, the charity could be named as the policy's beneficiary.

The full amount of the death benefit would qualify as a charitable gift in the year of death. Under the new rules, the gift can be used to offset 100 percent of Sheri's income in the year of death. If there is a portion of the gift that cannot be utilized in the year of death, the remainder can be carried back to the previous year.

A small annual outlay for the insurance premium will allow Sheri to provide a very large gift and save a significant amount of taxes in the year of her death. This strategy will also ensure that her children or other descendants will receive more than if the gift came out of the estate's assets.

Another benefit is that Sheri retains control of the policy. If she decides she wants to help out another charity, all she has to do is change her will or beneficiary designation.

If Sheri assigns the policy to a charity and has a change of heart later on, her only recourse would be to stop paying premiums on the policy. She would then have to apply for a new policy, which would be more expensive (assuming she is insurable at that time).

In the future, it is likely that more donors will continue to own the insurance policy and gift the death benefit rather than set up the charity as the owner and claim the premium payments as a charitable donation.

2. Gifts of publicly traded investments

Another rule change applies to the charitable donation of investments, such as mutual funds and publicly traded shares.

Normally, if you wanted to sell off some investments to raise cash for a charitable donation, the following consequences could occur:

- you might have to pay broker fees
- you could trigger a capital gain, which would result in the payment of some tax
- the tax on the investments could reduce the value of the credit arising from the gift to the charity

With the new rules, if certain types of property are gifted directly to a charity, only one-half of the resulting taxable capital gain has to be included in income. This provides a significant incentive to donate these types of properties if they have unrealized capital gains rather than sell them in order to fund the gift.

Let's assume Sheri—whom we mentioned earlier—has shares that she purchased for $1,000, and are now worth $2,000. She could sell those shares and gift the cash to her charity. The net tax result would be as follows:

Proceeds on Sale of Shares	$2,000
Cost Base	$1,000
Capital Gain	$1,000
Taxable Gain (50 percent)	$500
Tax (50 percent)	$250
Value of Charitable Credit (approximately)	$1,000
NET TAX BENEFIT	$750

As you can see, the value of the tax credit was reduced by the amount of tax on the capital gain of $250. The value of the tax credit works out to be $750.

Instead of selling the shares and gifting the cash, let's assume that Sheri gifts the shares directly to her charity. In this case, the tax payable on the capital gain is 50 percent less, as shown below:

Proceeds on Sale of Shares	$2,000
Cost Base	$1,000
Capital Gain	$1,000
Taxable Gain (25 percent)	$250
Tax (50 percent)	$125
Value of Charitable Credit (approximately)	$1,000
NET TAX BENEFIT	$875

As a result of the new rules, the tax benefit increases from $750 to $875. This is due to the lower inclusion rate for capital gains. And, you don't have to pay the broker fees.

There are some exclusions

Gifts of real estate and shares in private corporations are not eligible for the reduction in the inclusion rate for capital gains.

The federal government was concerned about valuation issues and limited the types of properties that benefit from these rules to publicly traded shares, as well as investments in mutual funds and segregated funds. There is a ready market for these types of assets, and values can be easily ascertained through the stock exchanges or newspapers.

The other interesting thing about these rules is that they are subject to a sunset provision. These rules are only in place until the end of 2001.

So, while these rules will apply to gifts made through a will, there is some uncertainty about how long they will remain in effect.

The federal government recently extended this beneficial tax treatment to employees who make a charitable gift of shares acquired under stock options. If certain criteria are met, the taxable inclusion that normally results from exercising a stock option will be further reduced by 50 percent. This will put gifts of shares acquired under certain stock options on the same tax basis as gifts of public securities.

It is also important to note that these rules do not apply to gifts of qualifying property made to private foundations. These are foundations that are normally established by large donors to disburse funds to other charitable foundations and organizations. This rule addresses a general concern about the use of private foundations as a means for wealthy individuals to reduce their tax bills.

3. Gifts of capital property

There have also been rule changes that apply to other types of property with unrealized gains. As previously mentioned, a person cannot claim charitable gifts exceeding 75 percent of net income in any given year.

Even though there is a five-year carry-forward provision for unused gifts, the income limit has created some barriers for individuals who want to gift appreciated property to charities. In certain situations, such gifts could trigger more taxable income than the charitable credit would cover. For example, assume you purchased a vacant parcel of land 10 years ago for $5,000. It has now become very valuable and is worth $100,000, and your church is looking for property to build on. Being the charitable type, you are prepared to donate the vacant lot to the church.

Let's look at the tax consequences arising from the donation of the vacant land. Assume that you have no other sources of income in the year. Here's how it breaks down:

Fair Market Value	$100,000
Cost Base	$5,000
Capital Gain	$95,000
Taxable Gain (50 percent)	$47,500
Tax Payable on Gain (50 percent)	$23,750
Allowable Donations (75 percent)	$35,625
Donation Credit (approximately)	$17,813
NET TAX PAYABLE	$5,937

Because of the 75 percent income limit on charitable donations, you cannot claim the full donation in the year the gift is made. However, you have to claim the full capital gain in the year you donate the property.

After taking into account the charitable credit, you still have a tax bill of almost $6,000. This isn't really the encouragement you need to gift the property to the church.

You are, however, allowed to carry forward the remainder of the charitable gift, which is about $65,000 (Fair Market Value—Allowable Donations), and claim it over the following five years. But if you have little in the way of taxable income, the carry forward will not be very useful. You want the credit this year to offset the capital gains.

The charitable sector drew this scenario to the attention of the federal government, and the government made some changes. Now, if a person donates appreciated property to a charity, there will be a further credit allowed in the year the gift is made equal to 25 percent of any capital gains or recaptured depreciation arising from the gift. This rule change applies even if the gift of capital property is to a private foundation.

Instead of claiming $35,000 as a charitable gift, you would now be able to claim an amount equal to the full taxable gain of $47,500. This would essentially offset all your gains and would reduce your carry forward of the excess charitable gift to $52,500 (which represents the difference between the charitable gift of $100,000 and the creditable gift of $47,500).

It is anticipated that these relaxed rules will encourage more people to gift capital property with appreciated gains to charities.

Put another policy in place

For some, it makes sense to use part of the tax savings resulting from the donation to purchase an insurance policy. This is a great way to replace some of the value of the gifted property, while still avoiding the payment of tax on the disposition of the property. And the life insurance proceeds would be tax-free to the estate.

4. Gifts to private foundations

There is one final rule change aimed directly at gifts to private foundations by small business owners. Here's an illustration.

Let's say David, a small business owner, wants to form a private foundation to distribute gifts to a number of different charities. As one of the directors, he would have a major say in how the funds are disbursed. Since most of David's wealth is tied up in his business, he might gift shares in his company to the private foundation instead of cash.

You'd think that David would want to be able to claim a charitable tax credit for the value of the shares gifted to the private foundation. But how would the charity ever realize the value of the shares that it owns? After all, the shares are not publicly traded, so there is no ready market. And what happens if the company runs into financial difficulty and the shares drop in value or become worthless?

Making good on the value

These are the same concerns that the federal government had with these types of arrangements.

Regarding the realization of the share values, there was usually an arrangement where the company would repurchase the shares upon the death of the shareholder. Often, the company would own insurance on the life of the shareholder that would be used to fund this repurchase.

The issue of a ready market is more difficult to deal with. Since the shares are not publicly traded, the value has to be determined by other means. The federal government was concerned that the value of the donated shares would be overstated to maximize the shareholder's charitable credit. And even if the shares are properly valued at the time the gift is made, the charity may realize much less for them if the company is not successful in the future.

Complications "R" us

To deal with these issues, the federal government has introduced some rather draconian tax legislation.

Under the rules as initially proposed, if David gifted shares or debt in his company to a charity (public or private), the charitable gift that normally arises would have been denied, unless the shares or debt were disposed of by the charity within five years of making the gift.

If the charity did dispose of the shares or debt within the five-year period, the value of the gift would be the lesser of the gift's value at the time it was made and the amount received by the charity for those shares or debt. If there was any decline in the value of the shares or debt, the value of the charitable donation would be reduced.

Here are some numbers to demonstrate this arrangement in action. Suppose David decided to gift $100,000 worth of shares in his company to a private foundation. Normally, he would be able to claim a charitable credit equal to 75 percent of his net income in the year. So, if David's income in the year exceeded $135,000, he would be able to claim a credit on the full $100,000.

Under the new rules, David would be denied the charitable credit unless the private foundation disposed of those shares within five years of receiving the gift. He could not claim a charitable credit unless the charity converted the shares or debt into cash.

But the gift of the shares would be a disposition for tax purposes. If the shares had a nominal adjusted cost base, the gift of $100,000 in shares would create an income inclusion of about $50,000.

The rules, as first proposed, would have allowed David to claim a capital gains reserve to offset any capital gains for a maximum of five years.

The gain would be taxable if the charity sold the shares within five years of receiving the gift, and there would be an offsetting charitable tax credit for the gift of the shares. The real kicker? If five years went by, David would have to pay tax on the capital gain, even if no charitable credit was allowed for the gift.

But all is not a loss

This proposal drew a lot of criticism from the charitable sector, and fortunately the government has somewhat modified its position. Under the revised rules, the donor will not have to worry about capital gains if the charitable donation is disallowed.

The federal government also introduced additional provisions that may allow an immediate charitable credit for gifts of shares to charitable organizations (other than private foundations) provided the donor is dealing at arm's length with the charity.

However, the restrictions on gifting debt of private corporations will remain. The net result is that gifts of shares in a small business to a private foundation and gifts of debt in a small business to any charity will not qualify for a charitable credit, unless the shares or debt is converted to cash within five years of receipt.

Like a lot of government tinkering, these rules complicate things for the donors and charities alike.

Another way to say you care

Charitable annuities offer yet another option in the gifting department. They can be a good idea in the right situation.

To elaborate, let's consider Doris, a 67-year-old woman with a variety of different investments that provide her with income. One of those investments is about $200,000 in Canada Savings Bonds. Doris is earning a 6 percent return on the CSBs, providing about $12,000 per year. She is in a 40 percent tax bracket, netting about $7,200 after tax.

Doris is considering donating the $200,000 in Canada Savings Bonds to a charity. In turn, the charity has agreed to provide her with an income of $8,400 per year for the rest of her life. This is known as a charitable annuity—the charity is providing Doris with a regular income in return for the donation of a lump sum.

Since she was making $12,000 before tax from the CSBs, this might not look like a good deal on the surface. However, Canada Customs and Revenue Agency will treat the $8,400 paid by the charity as a return on her original $200,000, so she doesn't have to pay any tax on this amount.

In effect, Doris will receive more income on an after-tax basis than had she retained the CSBs. She would also be entitled to a charitable credit for a portion of the funds that she gifted to the charity.

To figure out if any portion of a gift qualifies for a tax credit, and the amount of tax-free income that can be received under one of these programs, CCRA has set out administrative practices in Interpretation Bulletin IT-111R2, entitled "Annuities Purchased from Charitable Organizations."

Before she goes any further, she should see if any portion of the funds provided to the charity in return for the annuity will qualify as a charitable gift.

This is based on the life expectancy of the individual, as set out in the mortality table in the Interpretation Bulletin. In our example, the actuaries predict Doris will live until age 87, another 20 years.

If we multiply the number of years she is expected to live by the payments she is going to receive (20 x $8,400), the total equals $168,000. Since she is transferring $200,000 to the charity, Doris will be entitled to a charitable donation receipt for the difference of $32,000.

Also, since the payments are less than the amount transferred to the charity, the full amount of each payment is treated as a tax-free return of capital.

Is there a catch?

This sounds like a pretty good deal, and it is, but there are issues that need to be dealt with.

First of all, Doris should find out if the charity is self-funding the payments or passing on the risk to an insurance company through the purchase of an annuity. If the charity is self-funding, Doris needs to be comfortable with the long-term financial viability of the charity.

Doris also needs to understand that the payments from the charitable annuity will not be adjusted in the future, even if interest rates go up significantly. But perhaps the greatest issue is that Doris will give up control of the original capital, losing flexibility and depleting the value of her estate.

As usual, there are remedies

Instead of gifting the $200,000 to the charity, Doris might be better off using these funds to purchase a prescribed annuity from an insurance company. Based on current annuity rates, Doris would receive about $15,800 per year for the rest of her life.

Of this amount, about $5,900 would be taxable and the rest would be treated as a return of her original capital. She could then gift the taxable portion of the annuity payments to the charity, which would offset the taxes payable on this income.

This approach would give her about $9,900 after tax, which is more income than she would receive under the charitable annuity program. And, if her charitable intentions change in the future, she would have the option of keeping the full amount of the annuity payments or redirecting the income portion to another charity. A little more flexibility can't hurt.

While this approach does allow her to exert more control over the use of the funds, her estate would still be reduced by $200,000 due to the purchase of the annuity.

So, what can be done? Instead of taking the higher income, Doris could use some of the annuity proceeds to purchase a life insurance policy.

For example, she could purchase $50,000 of Term to 100 insurance and still have a higher income than what would have been generated through the charitable annuity. While she does not fully replace the $200,000, both Doris and her estate will be in a better position than going with a charitable annuity program.

In the next chapter

- Typical "in trust" accounts
- The real deal about trusts
- Trusts and tax treatments
- Trusts and the family
- The Canadian Education Savings Grant
- Trusts for shares in small business
- Trusts for special needs children
- Protecting your family from creditors

8

Don't just lie there—delegate

Most of us find it hard to ask others to do our bidding. But there'll come a time when you have to let go of the reins

WHERE LARGE SUMS OF
MONEY ARE CONCERNED, IT IS
ADVISABLE TO TRUST NO-ONE.
—Agatha Christie

Agatha Christie may be speaking from paranoia caused by delving too deeply into the criminal mind, but there's at least a grain of truth in her statement. But you cannot plan your estate without help from reliable, trustworthy people, especially if your estate is substantial.

You have to be able to trust someone to take care of things after you are gone. It stands to reason that any relative or friend with a fondness for the ponies or those "can't miss" investment opportunities should not be your first choice. They may not like it, but they'll understand.

Fortunately, most of us know at least one person that will always try to do the right thing—someone who will unflinchingly follow your directions, as well as the advice of those individuals you have assigned to administer your various trusts.

Many people are confused about trusts—what they are, what they represent, and what they can accomplish. In previous chapters, I've touched upon the role trusts can play—both while you are alive and after your death—in tax planning and the care of family members. Now, let's look at these arrangements in more detail.

How do you get formal trusts into place, and what can they accomplish? Here's the lowdown.

Inter vivos trusts versus testamentary trusts

Earlier, we discussed trusts in respect to will planning—remember testamentary trusts? These trusts receive property from an individual who has died.

When financial and estate advisers speak of a family trust, they are usually referring to an inter vivos trust. In these cases, the property comes from someone who is still alive—usually parents or grandparents trying to help their children or grandchildren. Despite this crucial difference, the formalities in setting up the two types of estates are very similar.

Putting everyone in their place

There are three parties to a trust arrangement:
- the settlor—who establishes the terms of the trust and transfers property to the trustee
- the trustee—who receives the property and assumes responsibility for dealing with it according to the settlor's directions as set out in the trust agreement
- the beneficiaries—who are entitled to the benefits of the trust property, including distribution of income and capital

Trustees are obligated to act in the best interests of the beneficiaries, in a reasonable and even-handed way. They can be held personally responsible if this duty is breached.

As a settlor, you can establish income beneficiaries, who are entitled only to distributions of trust income, or capital beneficiaries, who are entitled to distributions from the underlying capital of the trust. A beneficiary can be both an income and capital beneficiary.

A settlor can also grant the trustee complete discretion in the allocation of income and capital among various beneficiaries. In some cases the settlor can act as a co-trustee and can also be one of the beneficiaries of the trust.

In essence, trusts can be as flexible or as restrictive as you desire. The trust agreement should give the trustee the directions and powers necessary to carry out the expected duties.

The three certainties (not including death and taxes)

In order to create a valid trust you need three certainties:
- there must be certainty that the settlor intended to create a trust arrangement (this is best evidenced by a written trust agreement)
- there must be certainty as to the property that is subject to the trust—normally accomplished by the trustee becoming the registered owner of the trust property
- there must be certainty regarding who is to benefit from the trust arrangement (again, a written trust agreement is the best way to identify the beneficiaries)

"In trust" accounts

"In trust" accounts typically hold mutual fund investments for children. These arrangements are trying to replicate some of the tax benefits of family trusts.

However, the lack of a formal trust agreement leaves the door open for Canada Customs and Revenue Agency to challenge the validity of these vehicles. There are also other legal problems associated with "in trust" accounts.

Guidelines can be murky

A formal trust agreement sets out a fairly comprehensive list of powers for the trustee. In the absence of such an agreement, a trustee must rely on the common law and provincial legislation to define his or her powers. Depending on the province, the trustee's investment powers could be very limited.

In fact, mutual funds may not be permitted investments in some provinces. As well, the beneficiaries of "in trust" accounts will be entitled to the proceeds of the trust when they attain the age of majority. This may not be the intention of the parent or grandparent who establishes the "in trust" account. There is also the question of who becomes entitled to the funds in the event of a minor beneficiary's death.

Clearly, there are a number of issues that have to be addressed with "in trust" accounts. Given this potential for difficulties, why don't more people have a trust agreement prepared for them?

Unfortunately, the costs of having a lawyer draft a trust agreement may be prohibitively expensive where small amounts are involved. Even the most simple agreement will likely cost between $2,000 and $3,000 to set up.

If you are only putting a few hundred dollars a month into an investment account for your child, this is a difficult expense to justify from a tax-savings point of view.

Consequently, "in trust" accounts continue to be used despite their potential drawbacks.

Inter vivos trusts and the taxman

With family trusts, you need to consider the tax treatment of the settlor, the trust, and the beneficiaries.

Let's first consider the settlor's situation. Generally, the transfer of property from the settlor to the trustee will represent a disposition for tax purposes. The settlor will be considered to have disposed of the property at its current value and will have to pay tax on any gains. In turn, the trust will acquire the property at its fair market value. We will discuss a new exception to this general rule on page 129.

Depending on the terms of the trust agreement, an inter vivos trust generally has two options when it comes to earned income. The first is to distribute the income to the beneficiaries. Assuming the attribution rules don't apply, this income will be taxed to the beneficiaries at their marginal rates.

The income will also retain its character when paid out to a Canadian resident beneficiary. For example, if the trust allocated dividend income to the beneficiary, the beneficiary could claim the dividend tax credit. Similarly, only 50 percent of the capital gains allocated to a beneficiary are taxable.

The second option is for the trust to retain the income. A trust is considered a separate taxpayer and will pay tax on any income that is not taxable to the beneficiaries.

Unlike a testamentary trust, which pays tax at marginal rates, an inter vivos trust is automatically taxed at the highest marginal rate. So there is no tax advantage for an inter vivos trust to retain income that it earns on trust property, except perhaps to avoid or minimize federal or provincial surtaxes. The trick is to pay out the income to the beneficiaries, assuming they are in a lower tax bracket.

But another word of caution—if the beneficiaries of the trust include the settlor's spouse or children, you have to be concerned about the income attribution rules. Similar concerns may also arise if the settlor is a beneficiary.

If you transfer property to your spouse or minor children and they earn investment income, this income will be taxable to you. This rule prevents a person in a high tax bracket from shifting income to a family member in a lower tax bracket. For the purposes of these rules, a spouse includes a common law spouse where the parties have cohabited for at least a year, or there has been a child from the relationship.

These rules apply both to property transferred directly to your spouse or child, and to property indirectly transferred through a trust or certain other vehicles. If an inter vivos trust distributes income to a beneficiary who is the settlor's spouse or minor child, that income will be included in the settlor's income.

Right about now you're probably thinking, "I don't get it." An inter vivos trust must pay tax at the top rate on income that it retains. If the income is distributed to a spouse or minor child, that income will also be taxed to the settlor of the trust.

You may be correct in asking, "Why would someone go to the expense of setting up a family trust when there doesn't appear to be any tax advantages?" It's not quite as bad as it sounds. First, there are exceptions to the income attribution rules. And second, there are often non-tax reasons for establishing a family trust.

Trusts and the three Rs

One of a family trust's most important uses is financing the education of children and/or grandchildren. Let's examine a hypothetical situation to see how the inter vivos trust plays its role.

Anne, a widowed woman in her sixties, has a daughter with two young children. Anne also has a married son. He and his wife are expecting their first child. Concerned about the rising costs of post-secondary education, Anne would like to create a fund for the grandchildren who choose to go to university or college.

Anne could use any one of several approaches, including setting up a savings plan earmarked for the grandchildren, a Registered Education Savings Plan (RESP), or an educational trust for the grandchildren.

From a tax perspective, the savings plan is the least attractive—Anne will be responsible for tax on all the income earned by the fund. An RESP, on the other hand, offers the advantage of tax-deferred accumulation. Due to recent tax changes, these plans are also a lot more flexible. And if any of Anne's grandchildren go on to university, the income in the plan will be taxed to that child.

Using government leverage

One of the advantages of the RESP program is the Canadian Education Savings Grant. Under this program, the federal government will contribute an additional amount to the RESP equal to 20 percent of your RESP contribution each year, to a maximum of $400 per child. Assuming the RESP is started when the children are infants, this annual grant can accumulate to a tidy sum as the income keeps compounding.

If no children choose to pursue post-secondary education, today's RESP allows the transfer of funds to the sponsor's RRSP, to defer tax on the income, provided that there is RRSP contribution room available. If the plan is collapsed and the funds are not transferred to an RRSP, any investment income is taxable and subject to additional tax of 20 percent.

While this improved flexibility is certainly good reason to consider an RESP, these plans might not be the best course, especially for older individuals like Anne.

Since Anne is retired, she would likely not be able to take advantage of the RRSP transfer if the plan was collapsed. There are also restrictions on how much can be contributed to an RESP each year, and Anne would like to put the funds aside immediately. She also wants to ensure that her grandchildren can use the funds even if they don't go to university or college. Given these concerns, an inter vivos educational trust may be the best route.

Handing out the goodies

Here's how an inter vivos educational trust would play out. Anne would contribute a lump sum, say $100,000, into separate trusts for the grandchildren. She would be a co-trustee with her daughter and son under each trust.

The trustees would be permitted to make payments to the grandchildren to assist them with living and educational expenses. This is known as a discretionary trust—the trustees have discretion regarding when and how income or capital will be distributed. (This is to be contrasted with a non-discretionary trust, where the trustees are obligated to distribute a certain amount of the trust funds to specified beneficiaries on an annual basis.)

Why would Anne opt for this arrangement over setting up an investment fund for each grandchild? In both instances, she has to pay the tax on the income. With the investment fund, however, she avoids paying the legal and accounting fees associated with a trust.

But this is where you can take advantage of one of the exceptions to the attribution rules for minor children. These rules only apply to income earned on the investments that are distributed from the trust.

Income for these purposes does not include capital gains. So the trustees can select investments that primarily generate income in the form of capital gains—such as public shares, mutual funds, and segregated funds (the insurance industry's equivalent of mutual funds).

There are many mutual and segregated funds that have capital growth as their main investment objective. And there are many that can provide systematic withdrawals while still retaining the ability to compound and bolster the capital investment.

However, if the trust distributes interest or dividend income to the grandchildren, this income will continue to be taxed to Anne until the grandchildren reach the age of 18.

Also, since these are discretionary trusts, the capital gains actually have to be distributed to the grandchildren to be taxed in their hands. With minor children, this can be accomplished by making payments on behalf of the children. And very few children under age 18 would be in the top marginal bracket.

Where does the money go?

Until recently, the type of expenses a trust can pay on behalf of minor beneficiaries has been a source of considerable debate. Most professional advisers recommended that the funds be used to cover such expenses as vacations, summer camps, and private school tuition.

However, Canada Customs and Revenue Agency recently indicated that such payments could also be used to cover necessities of life, including food, shelter, and clothing. This significantly expands the type of expenses that can be paid for by a trust.

If the child or children decide not to enter the world of academia, flexibility in the use of the accumulated investments is very important.

If one of Anne's grandchildren chooses not to go to university or college, Anne will have to decide how she wants to deal with this situation under the trust agreement. She could specify that the funds are to be paid into the trust fund of another grandchild who is attending a post-secondary institution. Or she could choose to distribute the funds to the named beneficiary—either at the present time or later on. Anne herself could be one of those beneficiaries. She could go on a nice vacation or redirect the funds to another purpose.

This alone demonstrates the benefit of this type of program over a Registered Education Savings Plan.

More than meets the eye

There are other advantages to establishing a family trust. In Anne's situation, the trusts will continue to do what she intended even if she and the parents of the children become incapacitated or die.

The trust agreement allows for the appointment of replacement trustees and ensures the ongoing administration of the trust objectives. As well, by placing the funds in the trust, those assets will not be part of Anne's estate when she dies. Anne will not be taxed on any unrealized gains on the invested assets upon death, and there are no probate fees payable on the assets held in the educational trusts.

If she wanted, Anne could also distinguish between who gets the trust's income and who gets the capital. For example, she could specify that the income is to be used for the benefit of the grandchildren, but that her own children would ultimately receive the original capital that was contributed to the trusts.

Trusts for shares in small businesses

Family trusts are also an effective way for business owners to pass over control of their companies to their children.

Let's take a look at a hypothetical situation involving Joe, a small business owner. Joe has a significant tax liability associated with shares in his company. These shares are currently worth about $3.5 million. Assuming Joe holds on to these shares until death, and he is entitled to the $500,000 capital gains exemption upon death, he is looking at a tax bill in the range of $750,000, based on current values. As the value of the company increases, so will the potential tax hit.

Joe must also come to grips with who will run the business when he retires or dies.

Joe needs to reduce his future tax exposure and have some flexibility in selecting who will take over the business. A family trust is an integral part of this program.

As a first step, the shares in Joe's company, known as common shares, will be converted into preference shares with a value of $3.5 million. This is known as an estate freeze, because the value of the shares has been frozen at $3.5 million.

As part of this transaction, Joe will also utilize the capital gains exemption, increasing the cost base of his shares by $500,000. This is known as a capital gains crystallization. It allows Joe to lock in a higher cost base without paying any taxes, and avoids issues if the capital gains exemption rules are changed or the corporation's shares fail to qualify for the exemption in the future.

Changing the guard

This is where the family trust comes in. Joe wants all his children, and eventual grandchildren, to benefit from the growth of the business while he is alive. But he also wants to ensure that only the children who are active in the business will ultimately receive the shares.

Sounds like a complicated arrangement. And to some degree, it is. Let's look at Joe's family situation and circumstances to see how these issues can be resolved.

His daughter is very involved in the business and is doing quite well. He also hopes his youngest son, who recently dropped out of university, will eventually join the business. There is also the possibility that his eldest son might want to become involved somewhere down the line.

To create some planning flexibility, a family trust is organized. The beneficiaries include Joe, as the owner of the company, and his wife, plus their three children and any grandchildren.

Joe and his wife, together with a trusted professional—in this case their accountant—will act as trustees, and they must act by majority decision. The trust will borrow funds from a bank to subscribe for common shares in the company.

It is important that the trust does not use funds provided by the owner to purchase the shares or the income attribution rules may apply.

Who owns what

You should also note that the family trust does not control the company. Joe continues to control the company through his voting preference shares. He also has significant influence over the new common shares in his role as a co-trustee of the family trust.

The plan is for the company to pay dividends to the family trust. Those dividends could then be allocated to the children and grandchildren as income beneficiaries.

In the case of the adult beneficiaries, the income attribution rules do not apply. As for the minor beneficiaries, the rules in effect before 2000 include a specific exclusion from the attribution rules where the company's shares were qualifying shares of a small business corporation. In effect, this made it possible to do some income splitting with minor children where the property held by the trust consists of shares in a small business corporation.

However, the federal government has recently introduced new legislation that will negatively impact on this planning opportunity. The new rules provide that if a minor child receives dividends from a private corporation, either directly or through a trust, such dividend income will be taxed to that child at the top marginal tax rate. These new rules came into effect in 2000.

Unfortunately, these rules have eliminated a major income splitting opportunity for business owners. Nevertheless, some income splitting is possible with the spouse and adult children of the business owner, and there continues to be other tax and non-tax reasons for establishing a family trust.

Passing the torch

As for handing over the reins of the company, one of the first things Joe should get in place is company-owned life insurance. The insurance proceeds will be used to redeem Joe and his wife's preference shares upon the death of the survivor—in other words, when the last of this duo passes on.

This money will be distributed to those children who don't receive common shares in the company. The trustees of the family trust have discretion as to who will receive shares in the company. And, it is anticipated that those shares will ultimately be owned by the children who are involved in the business.

When all is said and done, the active children will control the firm, and the inactive children will receive cash.

Similar to a lot of planning strategies discussed earlier, this type of arrangement offers other benefits, such as a reduction in probate fees and deferral of capital gains taxes. The assets in the family trust are excluded from Joe and his wife's estate, and are therefore not subject to probate fees.

As an added bonus, the trust assets can be distributed to the capital beneficiaries on a rollover basis. This means that any capital gains accruing on the company's common shares will not be realized when the trust distributes them to the children.

This strategy also multiplies the use of the capital gains exemption for shares in a small business corporation. Each child who receives shares can shelter up to $500,000 of capital gains on a subsequent disposition of those shares.

By dealing with these issues ahead of time, you can avoid a lot of backtracking and most certainly a more costly, drawn out, and often bitter outcome.

Trusts for special needs children

Family trusts can be very useful where a disabled child is involved. In particular, a trust can be established to fund the special needs of that child.

If the child is a minor, you can minimize the impact of the attribution rules by investing in capital growth investments. And once the child reaches the age of 18, the attribution rules cease to apply. The use of a discretionary trust may also permit the child to take advantage of other government programs that provide financial assistance to disabled persons.

It is also easier to have income from a trust taxed to a disabled child. There is a specific provision that allows the trustee to allocate income to certain disabled children for tax purposes without actually distributing the income. I'll get back to this in Chapter 9.

Client confidentiality

If you have privacy and confidentiality concerns, family trusts can also be an important tool.

For example, you could choose to wait until death to distribute property through your will. However, once the will is probated it becomes a public document that anyone can access upon payment of the appropriate fee.

On the other hand, a trust document is totally private and only the parties directly involved need to be aware of its contents. Some people have established inter vivos trusts to protect their financial affairs from prying eyes.

Creditor protection

Many business owners and professionals establish family trusts to protect assets from personal creditors. Since the settlor gives up ownership interest in the assets held in a trust, creditors cannot seize such assets—unless it can be established that the trust was established primarily to defeat their claims.

A discretionary family trust can also protect beneficiaries against claims by their own creditors.

More issues of trust

Does the spouse of a beneficiary have any rights in respect of the trust property? That depends on the nature of the trust and the specific legislation in each province.

In certain provinces, family law legislation requires that the value of all assets acquired during marriage be shared equally.

If one spouse has only discretionary interest in a trust, assigning that interest any particular value will be difficult. So it may be possible for parents to gift assets to a child through a family trust and minimize claims arising from a marriage breakdown.

However, such protection likely does not exist if the child receives property from the trust or has a fully vested interest in the trust property.

Troubles you could face

I have mentioned some downsides of family trusts—the legal and accounting fees, and the income attribution rules. But that's not all. It is possible for shares in a private corporation to go off-side and cease to qualify as shares in a small business corporation. This can happen if more than 10 percent of the corporation's assets are not used in an active business. This would seriously impact trusts set up to hold shares in a private corporation.

If this occurs, the attribution rules would apply to the family trust in that and future years. The corporate attribution rules are quite onerous and would attribute income to the settlor even though no income is actually distributed to the trust's beneficiaries.

It is important to manage the status of the corporation to ensure that the exemption continues to apply to shares held in the family trust.

Time could run out

Another significant concern is the potential application of the 21-year deemed disposition rule. In order to prevent the use of inter vivos trusts as a means of avoiding the payment of capital gains taxes upon death for an indefinite period of time, this rule will deem a trust to have disposed of its capital assets every 21 years.

Let's consider Joe's situation as an example. His family trust acquired common shares in the company for a nominal amount. If we assume the trust remains in existence for 21 years, and the shares are worth $1 million at the end of that time, this rule will require the trust to pay capital gains tax on the $1 million accrued gain, even though the shares have not actually been sold.

How can the trust afford to pay almost $250,000 in taxes when it has no cash? It might be possible for the trust to borrow the money or dispose of some of its assets. But, usually, the shares are distributed to the appropriate beneficiaries just before the 21-year limit is reached.

As long as the beneficiaries are residents of Canada, such transfers can take place on a rollover basis. This would defer tax on the capital gains until the beneficiaries die or dispose of the shares.

There is yet another option, depending on the circumstances. The 21-year deemed disposition rule doesn't apply to life insurance policies. This approach involves setting up family trusts that own insurance on the lives of family members. These are exempt policies, so there is no income that needs to be reported on an annual basis. This removes any concerns about the income attribution rules.

Since the 21-year deemed disposition rule does not apply, these trusts can remain in existence as long as the policies remain in force, without any taxes being triggered.

Then, upon the death of the life insured, the tax-free death benefit can be reinvested or paid out to the beneficiaries in accordance with the trust agreement. As you can see, life insurance within a family trust can create some attractive tax and estate planning benefits.

Your alter ego

I indicated earlier in this chapter that the transfer of property by the settlor to a trust would result in a disposition of that property for tax purposes. This would create a tax problem if the property being transferred had significant unrealized capital gains.

Recently, the federal government introduced rules permitting the transfer of property to "alter ego" and "joint partner" trusts on a rollover basis. Assuming the proposed rules are enacted, these types of trusts will play an increasingly important role in estate planning.

How to qualify

An alter ego trust is a trust established after 1999 by a settlor who is 65 or older, for the exclusive benefit of the settlor during his or her lifetime. In other words, as long as the settlor is alive, no other person may receive income or capital from the trust.

A joint partner trust is also one created after 1999 by a settlor age 65 or older, but it is for the exclusive benefit of the settlor and his or her spouse during their lifetimes. For the purposes of these rules, spouses will include common-law spouses and same-sex partners.

Under either type of trust, other beneficiaries would be named to receive trust property after the death of the settlor or, if applicable, of the surviving spouse.

In most cases, the settlor's main objective will be to retain complete control over trust assets while alive. Upon death the trust assets will be distributed in a similar fashion to assets governed by the deceased's will.

Income tax considerations

As an inter vivos trust, an alter ego trust or joint partner trust will be taxed at the top marginal tax rate on all of its undistributed income. Income will be allocated to the settlor or, in the case of a joint partner trust, to the settlor and spouse. Income will be taxed at the recipient's marginal rate. In this regard, these trusts are taxed like any other inter vivos trust.

However, alter ego and joint spousal trusts do have one feature that sets them apart. The draft legislation provides that, contrary to the usual rule, there is no deemed disposition of property transferred to these trusts. Rather, the property will rollover to the trust for income tax purposes. In the case of alter ego and joint partner trusts, the deemed disposition is deferred until the death of the settlor, or the death of the surviving spouse. At that time, a deemed disposition will occur within the trust and, because this will be considered an inter vivos trust, tax will be payable at the top marginal rate on realized capital gains.

In light of the above, it appears that alter ego and joint spousal trusts do not present tax-planning opportunities. Income will not be taxed at a lesser rate, and unrealized gains will be taxed upon the death of the settlor or the settlor's spouse.

The main planning opportunities relating to these new trusts appear to be in the area of estate planning.

Planning opportunities

As discussed in Chapter 3, probate fees have been subject to well-publicized increases in Ontario, Nova Scotia and British Columbia. As a result, probate avoidance has assumed greater importance in estate planning.

The avoidance of probate fees through the use of inter vivos trusts has been gaining in popularity. Upon the settlor's death, property held in an inter vivos trust is not part of the deceased's estate and is therefore free of probate fees. Until now, Canada Customs and Revenue Agency's position was that a disposition arose on the transfer of property to such a trust—even where the settlor was the only beneficiary during his or her lifetime and even where the trust was completely revocable.

These income tax concerns generally meant that only property with no accrued gains could be transferred to an inter vivos trust without income tax consequences. This included cash and near-cash assets, such as term deposits and GICs, as well as shares and other capital property with no accrued gains.

The new rollover proposals mean that any property—including shares with accrued capital gains—may be transferred to an alter ego or joint spousal trust without income tax consequences. Upon the death of the settlor or the settlor's spouse, property will pass in accordance with the terms of the trust, not through the deceased's will. In this way, probate fees will be avoided.

This will be of particular interest to individuals with large investment portfolios that have significant unrealized capital gains and to shareholders of private corporations.

IN THE NEXT CHAPTER
- Family law issues
- Special needs dependents
- Substitute decision making
- More on marriage and divorce
- Partners in business
- Power of attorney
- Using a living will
- Dealing with debilitating illnesses

9

Indispensable instruments to orchestrate your intent

You would never enter into a contract without getting it in writing. The same applies when you organize your estate

A VERBAL CONTRACT
ISN'T WORTH THE PAPER
IT'S WRITTEN ON.
—Samuel Goldwyn

part from compromising the clarity of the English language, Samuel Goldwyn makes a very good point. Verbal contracts are all well and fine until a conflict or problem arises. And such situations always seem to arise. After all, it was Goldwyn, or one of his studio contemporaries, who told his secretary to make copies of all the documents they were throwing out, just in case they would be needed in the future.

If you think that a few carefully chosen words uttered to a family member or friend will suffice should you prematurely walk towards the light, think again. What can ensue from this approach to estate planning? Mild aggravation at best, and a whole litany of chaos and grief at worst. And this can happen even if you have a will in place.

Don't be mistaken—having your will prepared is a major step in planning your estate. But to make it truly effective, there are other issues that must be dealt with, sometimes within the will and sometimes through other legally recognized documents.

For many people, a simple and straightforward will should ensure a satisfactory resolution of their final wishes. However, for many families there are various complications, circumstances, and considerations to be covered.

There are three areas that can have a significant impact on how your will is structured and may require you to consider additional planning to maintain the integrity of your overall estate plan. They are:

- family law
- special needs dependents
- substitute decision making

While all three areas represent different issues, they may need to be interwoven to make your will truly workable.

1. Family law

No, this is not how you keep your family in line and make them do your bidding—although many parents would benefit from having the power to enact their own laws and collect fines for deviation from the rules.

But this is not a perfect world, and that is why the government has come up with rules of its own to ensure that marital conflicts can be resolved with some degree of fairness.

Take my spouse, please!

In today's society, a significant number of marriages end in divorce. Often, individuals involved will remarry or enter into common-law relationships. Some will have a second family. If you think everyday living can be complicated in these new blended families, just wait until you have to figure out who gets what in your will.

Even happily married people can experience problems down the road. Apart from the obvious death and taxes issues we've already dealt with, nothing in life is guaranteed—marriages included. It is important to understand the impact that changing family relationships may have on your estate plans. Not just now, but in the future.

Over the years, the law has changed significantly in the area of marriage breakdown. All provinces have legislation that governs the distribution of property when a marriage ends.

Some legislation, such as Ontario's Family Law Act, may also apply upon death. There can be significant differences from province to province regarding what types of property must be shared on marriage breakdown.

Ontario probably has the most comprehensive family law legislation, and we will spend some time talking about its impact. But whether you live in Ontario or another province, make sure your estate plan is reviewed by a lawyer in your particular part of the country. This will help you to understand the application of family law as well as dependent's relief legislation.

Share and share alike

The Ontario Family Law Act only governs the division of property between a legally married husband and wife. This legislation does not govern property rights arising from common-law or same-sex partnerships.

The rules provide that when legally married people separate or divorce, or one of them dies, a spouse can bring an equalization claim. Under an equalization claim, your spouse is entitled to 50 percent of the difference in each spouse's net family property (NFP).

Essentially, net family property is a measure of each spouse's increase in net worth during the marriage relationship. The one important exception is the matrimonial home. It will always be part of a person's NFP, even if it was acquired before marriage.

Let's look at a simple example. Mary and Bob were married at age 25 and separated at age 50. When Mary entered the marriage she owned property worth $10,000, and Bob owned property worth $15,000.

Upon their separation, Mary owned property worth $300,000 and Bob had property worth $650,000. After deducting the value of property owned at the time they were married, Mary's NFP would be $290,000, and Bob's would be $635,000.

If Mary brings an equalization claim, she would be entitled to 50 percent of the difference in their NFPs. That would be $635,000 less $290,000, which equals $345,000. That figure would then be divided in half, resulting in a $172,500 payout.

It is important to understand that Mary is not entitled to any specific property owned by Bob. He could borrow funds to pay the $172,500, or he could transfer some property to satisfy Mary's claim.

To make a bad situation worse, there could be substantial tax consequences if Bob needs to liquidate or transfer property to satisfy the equalization claim. When singers lamented, "Breaking up is hard to do," they really had no idea.

For couples who forgo that trip down the aisle or visit to city hall—as well as same-sex couples who, for the most part, do not enjoy the minimal benefits of common-law coverage—the prospect of a break-up can be even more involved.

Splitting up, the hard way

If your marriage survives the stresses of modern-day living, that's terrific. But no matter how well you and your spouse get along, the Family Law Act rules can apply upon death.

Similar to separation or divorce, the death of an individual gives the surviving spouse the right to make an equalization claim against the deceased's estate. The surviving spouse must choose between his or her entitlement under the will, or the equalization payment.

Your spouse would have six months from the date of your death to make this decision. If he or she makes an equalization claim, the estate must liquidate or transfer sufficient assets to satisfy that claim. Any remaining property is distributed in accordance with the terms of the will as if the surviving spouse predeceased the deceased. As you can see, this could have a significant impact on how property is distributed from the deceased's estate.

What can you do to avoid having your surviving spouse overturn the terms of the will by making such a claim? The simplest approach is to make sure your will provides your spouse with more than could be obtained under an equalization claim.

This requires estimating the net family property in the future, as well as the value of benefits to be provided under the will. This approach becomes significantly more complicated if you want to establish a discretionary spousal trust under the will.

In cases like these, your surviving spouse may prefer to make an equalization claim rather than wait for the trustees to determine his or her entitlement to benefits.

Other claim-countering implements

Another way to counteract the equalization issue is to rely on the special status given to life insurance and pension benefits. The Family Law Act provides that the proceeds of any insurance policy or pension plan owned by the deceased and paid to the surviving spouse will offset any equalization benefits owing to that person.

Let's go back to Bob and Mary. Instead of Bob and Mary separating, assume that Bob died upon reaching age 50. In his will, he left everything to their children. But Bob also owned an insurance policy for $300,000, with Mary as beneficiary. Mary is entitled to make an equalization claim of $172,500. This claim would, however, be fully offset by the insurance proceeds.

In fact, Mary would have to repay to the estate the excess death benefit of $127,500. So by ensuring the surviving spouse receives sufficient insurance proceeds or pension benefits upon death, you can bulletproof your estate from a family law claim.

Life insurance also has special status, as any death benefit received by an individual while married will be excluded in calculating that person's net family property.

Sign on the dotted line

In earlier times, a prenuptial contract was something that belonged in the realm of the rich and famous. Today, these types of premarital agreements have become more commonplace.

Most provinces recognize the ability of parties to enter into a marriage contract, with that document allowing the parties to override provisions of the applicable family law legislation, and set out the property rights of the spouses upon separation, divorce, and death.

Marriage contracts tend to be used more frequently in Quebec, and in second marriages where there is concern with protecting the rights of children from a prior marriage.

These contracts can also be limited to covering property rights arising only upon death. This will protect an individual's estate plan, while preserving each spouse's property rights on separation or divorce.

Your other partners

A growing number of Canadians are taking the entrepreneur route in their quest for job satisfaction and financial security. In effect, more and more Canadians are becoming business owners.

Without reservation, partners in business ventures should be aware of the potential impact of a spouse's property rights upon the death of a partner.

For example, consider the situation of three individuals who are equal shareholders in a business valued at $3 million. If one of the shareholders separated, this could trigger an equalization claim.

Although the separated spouse would not have a direct claim against the shares in the company, the shareholder might have to transfer or liquidate some or all of the shares to satisfy the spouse's claim.

This shows the importance of shareholders entering into a buy-sell agreement that contemplates this type of situation. The agreement could require the sale of the shares to the other share-holders at a predetermined price in the event of an equalization claim by the spouse of a partner. This would ensure that the shares do not end up in the hands of the separated spouse or other strangers to the business.

With so many marriages ending in divorce, this is probably more important than having buy-sell provisions governing the death or disability of a shareholder.

Obligations ad infinitum

Under family law, obligations to provide support continue after death. Marriage contracts, separation agreements, and divorce orders may also continue your obligation to support your spouse and/or children after your passing.

It is therefore important to review the terms of any separation or divorce agreement to see if support payments will be an ongoing obligation of your estate. If the answer is yes, this needs to be taken into account in your estate plan.

A recent court decision suggests that support requirements may continue after death, even if not originally contemplated by separation or divorce arrangements. Life insurance—coming to the rescue once again—is a very cost-effective way to take care of this ongoing liability. The estate or separated spouse can be designated as the policy's beneficiary, and the proceeds can be used to fund support payments.

If an agreement or divorce order does not specifically provide that support payments are to continue after death, it does not mean there are no further obligations.

Most provinces have legislation that gives certain family members the right to claim support from the estate of a deceased. In Ontario, for example, the Succession Law Reform Act provides that a dependent can apply to court for support out of the estate, if the deceased did not properly provide for that person under his or her will.

Separated or divorced spouses (including commom law spouses), as well as children, are entitled to support if they can demonstrate that they were dependent on the deceased. Other provinces have enacted wills variation legislation that allows family members to make a claim against the estate if the deceased failed to make adequate provision for the individual, even if that person is not a dependent of the deceased.

2. Special needs dependents

While this might not apply to most of the population, one of the most difficult and often heart-wrenching issues some parents have to contemplate is the future of dependents with special needs—children who require extra attention due to physical, emotional, or mental impairments.

An estate plan must take the special needs of these children into account. In most cases, the best course of action is the establishment of a trust to take care of their financial requirements.

One approach is to establish an inter vivos trust, particularly where the child is not able to properly manage his or her own financial affairs. The parents can establish a trust while they are alive and transfer property, such as cash or investments, to the trustees. Normally, the parents act as trustees, with alternate trustees appointed in the event a parent dies or can no longer act.

There are several benefits to this approach. It ensures that someone will properly invest the funds and use them for the benefit of the child, and the trust will survive the death or incapacity of the child's parents.

Maximizing special care

A disabled person's entitlement to government support programs is often dependent on their assets and income. Hence, a properly structured discretionary trust may allow that individual to continue to qualify for government assistance or other programs that might be too expensive for the family to fund.

The parents can also appoint different income and capital beneficiaries. If the disability is one that will shorten the child's life expectancy, the parents may wish all the income to go towards the support of that child, while ensuring that the capital eventually goes to other beneficiaries.

As is the case with other trust arrangements, there are probate fee savings, as well as the potential tax benefits of income splitting between the parents and special needs children.

For example, if the child is 18 years of age or older, any income earned by the trust can be taxed in the hands of the child instead of the parents. As well, if the child qualifies for the disability tax credit, it is possible for the trust to allocate income to the beneficiary for tax purposes without actually paying out such amounts.

This allows for more flexibility in deciding when to actually pay out income on behalf of the special needs child.

More tax savings possible

It is also possible to establish a discretionary trust for a special needs child under the parents' wills. This trust—referred to in previous chapters as a testamentary trust—can be funded with life insurance or other estate assets.

An additional benefit of this arrangement is that the income of a testamentary trust is taxed at marginal tax rates. As a result, income can be split between the trust and the special needs child to achieve an overall reduction in taxes.

There are circumstances where you may want to make a gift or bequest directly to a child with special needs. However, the following three conditions should guide that choice:

- the child has reached the age of majority
- there is no concern about the child's ability to manage his or her financial affairs
- access to government assistance is not an issue

In this situation, it may make sense to provide a gift or bequest through your will. This affords your child more independence, and avoids the costs involved in establishing and maintaining a trust.

If the child's ongoing financial needs are substantial, it may be appropriate to fund the gift with life insurance. This can preserve the remainder of the estate and avoid an unpleasant situation where other family members feel their inheritance is being used to support a special needs child.

If the child has not reached the age of majority, it is also possible to establish an insurance trust to hold and administer the proceeds. This is a type of testamentary trust designed specifically to hold insurance proceeds for minor beneficiaries. It is important that legal advice be obtained before implementing an insurance trust. The trustee must be given broad enough powers and discretion to carry out his or her duties as contemplated by the parents.

3. Substitute decision making

One of the most vexing aspects of human existence is our inability to stop aging. While many of us believe we can embrace aging with savoir faire and dignity, reality paints a different picture.

Thanks to new medical and technological advances, people are generally living much longer and often in better physical condition than earlier generations. Unfortunately, while the body may be willing, the mind is often not.

Diseases such as Alzheimer's and Parkinson's appear to be on the upswing, affecting the ability of many seniors to manage their personal and financial affairs. In the past, seniors could rely on family support or government assistance for nursing care.

But in today's fast-paced world, increased demands at work and home have reduced children's ability to respond to the needs of infirm parents. Furthermore, both the federal and provincial governments have significantly cut funding for hospital and institutional care.

As a result, there is an increased need to consider physical and mental incapacity when planning your estate. This can save an awful lot of work for your family and help preserve your personal wealth.

Who can you turn to?

There is a range of options when it comes to getting assistance with your decision making should your mental capacities begin to fail.

One is to transfer major assets, including your home and bank accounts, into joint ownership with your adult children. Some people are very comfortable with this arrangement and find it quite workable.

However, since you would normally make this arrangement before your capacities fail, it could restrict your ability to deal with these assets while still healthy. It could also have negative tax implications.

Alternatively, you could set up an inter vivos trust to hold your assets, making yourself both trustee and beneficiary. If you become incapacitated, one or all of your children could step in.

Depending on how the arrangement is structured, there may be tax implications on transferring property to the trust. You must also consider the costs associated with set up and maintenance. But with the new alter ego and joint partner trust rules, discussed in Chapter 8, this may be a more attractive option in the future.

Power sharing, family style

As important as your will is, equal importance should be given to a complementary document—a power of attorney. This document legally provides a trusted individual with the power to act on your behalf if you are unable to do so yourself.

The individual chosen for this role is usually a close family member, such as a spouse or common-law partner. For our purposes here, we will presume that your loved ones have your best interests at heart.

Many people think that a power of attorney is a good idea only for older individuals who fear that mental and physical frailty is just around the corner. That's a dangerous preconception. Even younger individuals with a modest estate—and especially if they are married or have children—should consider executing a power of attorney. Many healthy people in the prime of their life have been struck down and left helpless due to a debilitating illness or accident.

The pros and cons

Now that you're convinced that a power of attorney is just the thing to ensure peace of mind, there are a lot of issues to consider. The least of these is cost—a power of attorney is relatively inexpensive to put in place.

In the past, powers of attorney were invalid once the donor became mentally incapacitated. In a twisted sort of way, this undermines the reason for drawing up the document in the first place. Now, however, almost all provinces have legislation that allows you to provide that a power of attorney will continue to be effective even upon incapacity. This is known as an "enduring" power of attorney, and the benefit is that you do not give up ownership of any of your assets.

For many people, the thought of handing over the reins while still alive is quite nerve-wracking. What if that person you thought you could trust decides to access your funds, buy a new Rolex, and take off on a Caribbean cruise?

There are some inherent risks any time you turn over your personal authority to another person, but these can be managed in several different ways.

First, you should only appoint an attorney (in other words, your agent) whom you trust and who has demonstrated sound financial judgement over the years—the same criteria you would use in selecting an executor. In fact, it might be wise to appoint the same person as both attorney and executor to ensure that he or she is sensitive to your estate plan.

It is also possible to place restrictions on the powers that can be exercised by the attorney. For example, the power of attorney may be limited to dealing with a specific bank account or closing the sale of a house. You can restrict the attorney's investment powers or limit the power of attorney so that it is effective only upon your becoming mentally incompetent. This is known as a "springing" power of attorney, and it ensures that endowing someone with these powers doesn't necessarily mean they have carte blanche with your property.

In most situations, however, it is better to provide broad powers and avoid the need for the attorney to apply to court for directions and an interpretation of his or her powers.

Who says I've lost it?

At this point, you may well be asking yourself who determines the quality of your mental state.

The most common procedure is to specify in the power of attorney that your personal physician has to examine you and provide a letter stating that you are not capable of managing your financial affairs.

As well, you can have your financial adviser, accountant, lawyer, or other trusted professional hold on to the actual power of attorney document. Once this person has been provided with your doctor's letter, then the family member you have selected can access the power of attorney.

This is one way to protect yourself from any suspect dealings, while still ensuring that your attorney can quickly step in and take care of your financial affairs if you are unable to do so.

When the courts get involved

Individuals who fail to execute a power of attorney and are unable to deal with their financial affairs still have some protection.

Most provinces have legislation that appoints a government official, normally referred to as the Public Trustee, to oversee the administration of a person's financial affairs if that person is found to be mentally incompetent. Subsequently, a court order may be required to allow a family member to take over as guardian.

In Ontario, for example, the Public Guardian and Trustee will step in and take control of a mentally incompetent person's assets. A family member can then apply to replace the Public Guardian and Trustee as statutory guardian.

The Public Guardian and Trustee may require that the family member post a bond as security for the assets. If statutory guardianship is not available or appropriate, anyone, including a family member, can apply to court to have the person declared incompetent. He or she may then seek appointment as guardian of the person's property.

During this process, the incapable person's financial affairs may be in limbo, and the ensuing result could be economic hardship and/or the erosion of asset values. So while the government and courts can work to assist an incapacitated individual, having a power of attorney on standby means that this individual's affairs can be handled properly and promptly.

Being of sound mind, so far

There are other things to keep in mind when preparing your power of attorney. It is very important to inform the person you are considering and ensure that he or she is willing to act as your attorney. This person must be made aware of the legal obligations he or she would be assuming if you become incapacitated. For example, this person has a fiduciary duty to always act in your best interest.

There may also be statutory duties imposed on the attorney to provide regular accounting for the assets or to consult with you and the rest of your family on financial matters. This person must be aware of your wishes regarding ongoing charitable gifts and financial assistance for any descendants, if applicable.

To avoid possible conflicts, you could consider appointing joint attorneys, or alternate attorneys. This is also effective if the person who is appointed dies or becomes too ill to act.

Caution should be exercised if you are considering using a power of attorney kit. Much like will kits, these preprinted forms may not properly take into account your particular needs. Also, the requirements and wording of an effective, enduring power of attorney can vary from province to province. The best approach is to have a lawyer prepare your power of attorney. He or she is in the best position to guide you through all the options and ensure that nothing important is omitted.

Unlike the preparation of a will—which is still a fairly reasonable legal cost—a power of attorney is a real bargain. Legal fees for simple powers of attorney are in the $100 range. This is a minor cost when you consider the problems that can arise if the power of attorney is not valid once you are incapacitated, or your attorney has to go to court to clarify his or her powers and obligations.

Changing that sound mind

A power of attorney might be drawn up by an individual, or suggested by younger family members, when signs of incapacity are becoming evident. But many people have their powers of attorney prepared long before the documents might be put into play.

That's a smart move, but it also presents a challenge. Many years could elapse between the time that you draw up the papers and the time that your attorney might have to use them.

In that period, several things could transpire. Your attorney might:

- move away, making it difficult to handle your affairs from a distance;
- become estranged from you;
- have too many other pressing family- or work-related issues to deal with;
- demonstrate unsound judgement in handling other issues;
- become involved with issues of a criminal nature.

With any financial plan, estate plan, or insurance coverage, you have to review and revise from time to time. The power of attorney is no different. If the person you have appointed can no longer do the job, you have to make a change. The first step is to revoke the existing power of attorney.

This shouldn't be a problem, but beware—a power of attorney that is provided for a specific purpose, such as selling a property, will generally be irrevocable. This type of power of attorney will terminate when the transaction is completed. However, general purpose powers of attorney, including enduring powers of attorney, are normally revocable, and the process is fairly simple.

As long as you are mentally capable, you can revoke a power of attorney by communicating your intent to the attorney. Some provinces require the revocation to be communicated in writing and may require that your signature be witnessed.

147

You will also have to notify all the people who may have acted under the power of attorney in the past, such as your financial institutions and investment advisers. The execution of a new power of attorney will also normally revoke an existing power of attorney, unless a contrary intent is expressed.

It is important to note that a power of attorney generally ceases to have effect upon your death. At this point in time, the executor of your will takes control of your assets. The death or incapacity of your attorney will also result in the termination of the power of attorney, unless a joint or substitute attorney is named in the document.

It's not just the money

So far, we have examined how to ensure that proper financial decisions are made regarding your property should you become mentally incompetent. You should also be concerned about who will make decisions regarding your personal care if you are incapable of doing so.

Over the last five years, most provinces have passed legislation to allow the appointment of another person to make decisions governing your personal or health care. In Ontario, for example, you can appoint a power of attorney for personal care. The attorney can make decisions regarding both personal and health matters if you are declared mentally incompetent. In other provinces, such as Manitoba, Prince Edward Island, and Newfoundland, legislation allows the appointment of a proxy or representative to make health care decisions if you become incompetent. British Columbia and Alberta have enacted similar legislation.

The legislation in each province specifies when the appointment becomes effective and what types of health care decisions can be made. As much as possible, the attorney is expected to consult with the incapacitated person and other family members in respect to health care decisions. The attorney should keep extensive records of health care decisions made on behalf of the incapable person.

If you haven't made this type of arrangement, most provinces have legislation that dictates who can make health care decisions if you are incapable. For instance, if you have a serious car accident and fall into a coma, family members are normally entitled to make health care decisions on your behalf.

If you remain comatose for an extended period, resulting in an ongoing need to make personal and health care decisions for you, either a family member or the Public Trustee will need to apply to court to be appointed as your guardian.

Eschewing heroic efforts

Yet another document is playing more of a role in health care matters today. It is known as a living will. This type of declaration is currently recognized under the laws of British Columbia, Ontario, Manitoba, and Quebec.

A living will allows you to indicate your wishes regarding the types of medical treatment that should be administered if you are unable to provide consent to treatment. For example, through a living will it is possible to indicate that you do not want to be kept alive by artificial means or heroic efforts. This is particularly relevant for individuals who are terminally ill.

For those who wish to draw up a living will but reside in a province that does not recognize such documents, all is not lost. There are court decisions that have recognized the validity of living wills, even though the jurisdiction has not enacted legislation sanctioning them.

And even if the document is not legally binding, a living will can provide valuable directions to family members and medical professionals concerning your wishes for medical care. In most situations, this document would be very persuasive in determining the type of treatment to be administered.

Making the most of it

The last few years of a person's life can be the most intensive and costly in terms of medical and day-to-day care. Debilitating mental and physical conditions can persist for years, easily eroding both financial security and a substantial estate.

Again, insurance can come to the rescue. Critical illness insurance is one product that is relatively new in Canada and has been a big seller in other countries as well. It provides financial protection should you suffer a disabling critical illness.

If you are diagnosed with certain critical illnesses—such as heart attack, stroke, or cancer—and survive for a period of 30 days, this type of insurance will provide funds to assist with expenses arising from the illness and to replace lost income.

Critical illness insurance differs from disability insurance in several fundamental respects:

- the payment is usually made in a lump sum rather than in monthly instalments
- benefits are payable even if the insured recovers completely from the illness
- perhaps most importantly for older clients, coverage can extend past age 65 and into retirement

The longer the coverage period, the more likely you will suffer a covered illness and subsequently receive benefits. Of course, the premiums for these plans increase based on age and the length of coverage.

There are some variations among products, but most cover a dozen or so illnesses, including heart attack, stroke, cancer, paralysis, or the need for organ transplants.

It is also possible to use the benefits under a critical illness policy to pay for medical care outside of Canada. With medical cutbacks in Canada, plus lengthy waits for elective treatment, more and more Canadians want the option of going to the United States. Of course, the costs can be prohibitive, and insurance is the only fiscally sound way to pursue this health care option.

In for the long haul

There are few among us who have not experienced the emotional and financial drain of having a family member who requires ongoing medical attention. The impact can be an overwhelming burden on even the closest of kin. While no one wants to burden their family in this way, most of us don't have the financial resources to afford good-quality private home or institutional care on a long-term basis.

Suppose an elderly person suffers a major heart attack and needs to be admitted to a nursing home. If a private room is required, it could easily eat up more than $2,000 a month. At that rate, it wouldn't take long to deplete the average Canadian's estate. If that person wanted to stay at home, the cost of a private nurse could be even more significant.

In the past, the family would have accepted this cost, recognizing that their mother or father were not going to have as large an estate to pass on. In many of these situations, the family members may have had to subsidize these costs.

Now, that burden can be eased somewhat via an insurance product specifically designed to cover the additional expenses arising from the need for long-term care. Basically, you purchase a predetermined level of benefits that will help cover the additional costs of home care or institutional care.

For example, you can purchase benefits that will cover costs up to about $300 per day, which will be paid over a predetermined period of time. Of course, the higher the daily benefit, or the longer the payout period, the higher the premium. In the long run, however, the premium is much more cost effective than funding the cost of care out of savings.

This particular benefit becomes payable if the insured is chronically ill, suffers from cognitive impairment, or cannot perform certain functions that are referred to as activities of daily living. This would cover tasks such as eating, bathing, toilet activities, and moving about.

Not only does this product provide peace of mind, it also protects your estate plan by ensuring the assets are not unduly depleted by the costs of long-term care.

IN THE NEXT CHAPTER
- Estate planning for business owners
- Using the small business deduction
- Pros and cons of salary versus dividends
- How to bump up the RRSP
- Your family as company directors
- Capital gains exemptions
- Business succession planning
- Involving your family
- Freezing your estate
- Putting trusts to work
- The importance of your will
- Buy-sell agreements
- The versatility of insurance

10
Taking care of business

More and more Canadians
are becoming business
owners. And that can create
a lot of estate planning
dilemmas

WHENEVER YOU SEE A
SUCCESSFUL BUSINESS,
SOMEONE ONCE MADE A
COURAGEOUS DECISION.
—Peter Drucker

Inertia is one of the greatest forces to exert itself on human behaviour. True, it keeps us grounded—if that's how you want to define the lack of movement—but it also keeps us from making decisions, dealing with issues, and making progress.

Peter Drucker is right—success does come down to making a decision and having the courage to act on it. It is, essentially, the ability to look at the factors in play and tackle the ones that can trip you up.

Successful business owners know, just like those of you with sound financial and estate plans, that intelligent preparation can significantly improve the odds in your favour.

A lot more on the line

Estate planning can involve a multitude of components, even for people with modest assets. For business owners, a whole new set of issues can crop up when considering ways to integrate their enterprise into the complete estate picture.

Business owners can operate in any one of the following three ways:

- Sole proprietorships—the business owner carries on business in his or her own name, and has full personal ownership and risk in the enterprise. Many business consultants are sole proprietors.
- Partnerships—two or more business owners band together to assume personal ownership and risk in the business enterprise on a joint or common basis. Most lawyers and accountants work in formal partnership arrangements.
- Corporations—two or more business owners form a separate legal entity, known as a corporation, to carry on the business. Because they are only at risk for the capital contributed to start up the business, they are able to insulate themselves from personal liability. Many retail and manufacturing businesses are incorporated.

For the purposes of this chapter, we will focus on estate planning for shareholders in private corporations.

Private corporations are not listed on a public stock exchange and are not controlled by a public company. Most provinces limit the number of shareholders in a private corporation to 100 or less. Because the shares are not publicly traded, private companies are subject to less regulatory scrutiny than public companies. For example, they don't have to publish an annual report or provide a prospectus to those interested in purchasing shares.

In addition to different corporate regulations, public and private corporations and their shareholders are also subject to different tax rules.

The federal government assumes that shareholders of public companies are not actively involved in their operations and deal at arm's length with the management. The government also assumes that public companies have access to capital through the stock markets.

As a result, other than the dividend tax credit, there is little attempt to provide tax advantages or integration of tax benefits to shareholders of a public company.

On the other hand, the government does recognize that it is risky to invest in a private corporation and that these companies can find it difficult to raise capital. To address this situation, the federal and provincial governments have enacted tax measures designed to minimize any adverse tax consequences associated with earning income through a private corporation. There are, in fact, many tax advantages to carrying on a business through a private company.

Small business deduction

One of the main tax advantages of conducting business as a private corporation is that the first $200,000 of active business income is entitled to the small business deduction. Even income between $200,000 and $300,000 is subject to a favourable tax rate, although not quite as favourable as on the first $200,000.

This reduces the effective rate of federal tax from approximately 28 to 13 percent. When provincial taxes are included, the tax payable on the first $200,000 of active business income ranges between 15 to 22 percent across Canada.

This income will be taxed further when paid out as dividends to the shareholder. But as long as the money is retained by the corporation, there is a substantial tax-deferral opportunity for shareholders in a higher marginal tax bracket.

Salary versus dividends

Small business owners need to examine the total tax burden on income earned through the company and distributed to themselves as shareholders or employees.

For example, let's look at a company with net earnings of less than $200,000. Suppose the owner was receiving all of that income as salary. He or she thought this was a good approach, since it eliminated any tax in the company. Unfortunately, once in the owner's hands, much of the income is subject to tax at the top marginal rate. As well, the company has to remit payroll taxes on the salary. Clearly, this scenario is not the most advantageous. That's why a business owner should have a good tax adviser. A better approach is to figure out what the business owner needs to live on comfortably and pay that out regularly as dividend income. Although this means the corporation will pay tax on all its income, the tax rate will be lower as a result of the small business deduction.

Keep in mind that the business owner has to pay tax on the dividends. But he or she may also claim a dividend tax credit that will reduce the overall tax bill. The net effect? The owner can defer taxes by leaving some money in the company, while the overall personal tax bill will be reduced by paying out income in the form of dividends.

And, the money retained in the company reduces its reliance on bank financing and strengthens its cash flow position.

No earned income, no RRSP?

A major disadvantage of paying out business income as dividends is that it does not qualify as "earned income." As such, if the person has no other sources of income, he or she cannot channel money into an RRSP. For this reason, most accounting professionals recommend a mix of salary and dividend income so some RRSP contribution room is created.

Also, if that active business income rises over the $200,000 to $300,000 mark, the owner will definitely want to pay it out as salary since this income does not receive the small business deduction.

Business owners also have the option of paying salary or dividends to other family members, although family members must also be shareholders to qualify for dividends. For example, an owner's spouse can receive a salary for his or her services. This income falls outside the attribution rules and is taxed at the spouse's marginal tax rate, which should be lower.

This also creates the opportunity for the spouse to contribute to an RRSP, as well as accumulate non-registered investments. A business owner could also employ his or her minor children during the summer and holidays, and pay them a reasonable salary. Now, an owner's idea of a reasonable salary might differ drastically from that of Canada Customs and Revenue Agency. If CCRA feels the salary is unreasonable, they will deny the deduction of the "unreasonable" portion of the salary for the business. Professional advice will allow you to avoid raising any red flags with CCRA's auditors.

Directors' fees

Directors' fees offer another income splitting opportunity. Even if the owner's family members are not employed by the business, it is possible to elect them as directors of the company.

Canada Customs and Revenue Agency will allow the company to deduct reasonable fees paid to family members who act as directors, as long as they are at least 18 years of age.

This allows for the distribution of corporate profits to family members who are in a lower tax bracket and creates RRSP contribution room for them. Of course, in their role as directors, the family members should participate in board meetings and meet their legal obligations to the corporation.

What's reasonable to CCRA?

You have to be careful about how far you push these things. CCRA will take a dim view of arrangements that appear to siphon a large chunk of cash out of a company on a tax-advantaged basis. Again, get sound accounting expertise on your side. Paying family members director fees in the $5,000 to $10,000 range, and perhaps more in some circumstances, is usually quite acceptable.

Capital gains exemption

The capital gains exemption for shareholders of private corporations provides another area of tax savings. This can be a very significant aspect of estate planning if the owner's shares are transferred to his or her surviving spouse.

But there are several flies in the ointment. First, certain conditions must be satisfied for the shares to be eligible for this exemption. The main condition is that a majority of the company's assets must be used in an active business in the two-year period prior to their disposition and that 90 percent of the assets must qualify at the date of disposition.

If a business operation is wound down, this condition may no longer be satisfied and the exemption will be lost. There are also no assurances that this exemption will continue into the future. Given these potential problems, many tax professionals are recommending that their small business clients enter into a transaction referred to as a capital gains crystallization.

A crystallization permits the shareholder to "lock in" the benefits of the capital gains exemption without actually disposing of his or her interest in the company. This is accomplished by exchanging shares for two different classes of shares on a tax-free basis. The cost base of one class is increased by $500,000, and the resulting capital gain is sheltered by the exemption.

Another way to proceed with a crystallization is by transferring shares into a holding company. There is a provision of the Income Tax Act (section 85) that governs the transfer of property, including shares, to a corporation. As long as the individual receives shares in the new corporation as consideration for the transfer, he or she can, within certain limits, specify the transfer price. Under this transaction, the cost base of the new shares will be increased by $500,000. Again, the capital gains exemption is utilized to offset the resulting capital gain.

In both situations, the business owner continues to control the corporation, but the cost base of his or her shares has now been increased by $500,000. This will also reduce the shareholder's exposure to capital gains on the subsequent disposition of those shares.

The pros and cons

The benefit of the first method, which is referred to as a share reorganization, is two-fold: the owner does not go to the expense of setting up a new company, and the company itself retains a simple structure.

The benefit of the second technique, involving a holding company, is that new shareholders can be brought in without receiving a direct interest in the operating company. But using a holding company complicates things if the shareholder wants to sell the operating company.

To allow the shareholder to take advantage of the higher cost base, the purchaser would have to buy the shares of the holding company. This means that the holding company should not acquire other assets or take on liabilities that are not related to the operating company. There are also valuation issues to address if there is a transfer to a holding company.

But there is a downside to crystallization—a major concern that can be overlooked by tax professionals when advising clients. This concern relates to alternative minimum tax (AMT), which was introduced to ensure that high-income taxpayers could not take undue advantage of certain deductions in order to avoid paying taxes.

Under the AMT, a secondary tax calculation adds certain deductions back into income. One amount that is added back is a portion of a capital gain that is normally tax-free on the disposition of capital property.

It is possible, then, that a person undertaking a crystallization could have no regular tax liability but could end up paying alternative minimum tax.

Normally, this tax is refunded in future years, but it can create cash flow problems. If the AMT is a concern, it might be advisable to stagger the crystallization over several taxation years to minimize its impact.

No family limit on exemption

Since every taxpayer is entitled to the $500,000 capital gains exemption—provided they own qualifying shares in a company—it is extremely beneficial from a tax perspective to have as many family members as possible holding the shares. This will multiply the benefit of the capital gains exemption.

The other thing to remember is that the $500,000 capital gains exemption is only available to shareholders of incorporated businesses or on qualified farm property. Individuals who carry on business as sole proprietors or partners are not eligible for this exemption on the disposition of their interest in the business, unless it is a qualifying farming business.

However, the owners of these businesses can use section 85 of the Income Tax Act to transfer their business assets into a corporation on a tax-deferred basis in return for shares. By doing this, they benefit from the capital gains exemption, as well as the small business deduction and limited liability available through corporations.

Capital gains rollover

The federal government has introduced new proposals that will provide small business owners with a tax-free rollover of capital gains on the transfer of qualified investments from one small business to another.

For example, let's say that Joe, a small business owner, disposes of shares in a private corporation and realizes a capital gain. Up to $2 million of this gain can be deferred if Joe reinvests the proceeds in newly issued shares of certain private corporations.

These rules are designed to improve access to capital for start-up small businesses and offer a significant tax advantage to owners who reinvest proceeds from the sale of their shares.

Business succession planning

Once your business is humming along and you are taking advantage of all the tax options available to shareholders, you have another big challenge to face—other than an economic recession. How do you handle your company as you age, face retirement, and receive your pink slip from the great game of life?

All in the family

The prospect of retirement can be quite a polarizing ride of emotions. On one hand, there's the elation of eliminating that agonizing commute, no more work-related hassles, and all the time in the world to pursue your precious interests. But along with these perks comes the thought of entering your golden years with your career, which once defined you, becoming a distant memory.

For business owners, this dichotomy is even more pronounced. Yes, you get to spend more time with your family doing what you want to do; but this is countered by the loss of the work you put so much effort into. And, you've given up control of what is basically your creation.

The business of retiring can be awfully bittersweet—and fraught with all sorts of personal and financial crises if not handled with care. There are plenty of examples in the Canadian business world of founders who pass a business down to the children, and end up with a mess of squabbling and family estrangement.

A family affair

While the need for succession planning may be readily apparent, the personal dynamics of a family business are often overlooked or minimized. This can, after all, be complicated: you are trying to come to terms with a process that will eventually see you give up control of your business.

The prospect of retiring can be quite frightening. A business provides a sense of accomplishment and self-worth. However, retirement does not necessarily mean that the owner can't have an ongoing role in the business's success, especially if the firm is kept in family hands.

One of the first steps in the process is for the business owner and his or her spouse to assess their financial and personal goals for the future—including the big decision of who will run the business once retirement rolls around.

In the case of a private company, turning control over to the children might seem to be a pretty straightforward decision. But it's not always the wisest move—especially if it provokes dissension amongst the siblings or other relatives who might be involved.

If any of your children were involved with the company before your retirement, they would appear to be a logical choice—continuity counts. After all, if you were responsible for negotiating with the suppliers and banks, and making all major business decisions, chances are good that your son or daughter participated in these discussions. If this is the case, these business relationships should be able to weather the restructuring.

But suppliers, banks, clients, and even employees all have a vested interest in the status quo, and sometimes balk at major changes in company management.

If you have identified your successor—and this should be done with a fairly substantial timeline—get that person more involved in key business decisions. Not only will this allow your successor to gain valuable experience running the business, it will also enhance his or her relationships with suppliers, bankers, customers, and employees.

Everyone's nose in joint

Should you choose only one of your children to occupy the president's seat, the impact this could have on your other children will be a major concern. Some people feel it best to distribute company shares to all of the children and let them sort out the management issues. For the most part, that's really poor strategy—and a surefire recipe for conflict.

Children who are not active in the business will have a totally different set of priorities from those who remain involved. The non-active children would normally be interested in dividend income or even the eventual sale of the business at a profit. On the other hand, children active in the business would likely want to reinvest income to finance growth or reduce debt.

As owner, you might have to find an approach that will allow the children who are involved in the business to have an ownership stake while also ensuring that others receive a fair share, too.

The tribal council

A sensible first approach to the succession issue is to call a family meeting with your estate planner, your children, and your children's spouses. At this gathering personal, financial, and business considerations can be assessed, and family members can raise any questions or concerns.

For example, what happens if none of your children are involved in the business right now, but one does show some interest in running it in the future?

Clearly, he or she doesn't currently have the necessary skills and knowledge to take over from you. But that could change before you retire. In this type of situation, you could establish criteria that your child would have to meet within a certain time period in order to be considered as a possible successor.

This could include obtaining a business degree, gaining outside work experience, and assuming jobs with increasing responsibility within the business. You might want to retain a business consultant, or establish a committee, to provide an independent review of his or her performance and readiness to take charge.

If the criteria you established isn't met, it would be time to look for other candidates or sell outright. There may be employees who are interested and have the financial means to purchase the business.

You could also consider appointing an interim president to run the business until a suitable purchaser could be found.

No coffee at this CAFE

As you can see, there is much more to succession planning than a knowledge of the Income Tax Act. You and your advisers must be prepared to deal with the personal issues of business ownership. If your plan fails to address these issues, it is destined for failure.

Since no two situations are quite alike, it's sometimes helpful to brief yourself on some of the issues and their possible solutions. There are a number of organizations, such as the Canadian

Association of Family Enterprise (CAFE), that run programs that focus on the human dynamics of a family run business and succession planning.

To illustrate the point, let's look at the options faced by a typical business owner and his family. These strategies can be used for succession planning with most small business owners.

The ballad of John and Mary

John has worked hard for several years to build up his home construction business. He is pondering retirement, thinking later rather than sooner. His wife, Mary, would like it the other way around. He has three adult children, one of whom is currently working for the firm.

John owns all the common shares in his company, which are worth $3.5 million and have a nominal cost base. He has not utilized any of his $500,000 capital gains exemption.

Here's what John and his wife would like to accomplish:

- retain control of the business, pass ownership to any of the children who are active in the business at the time he retires, and provide each child with a fair share of their estate
- minimize current taxes and those that arise upon death
- ensure an appropriate level of retirement income for themselves
- create an education fund for their grandchildren

This couple has just cleared a major hurdle: they have established their goals. Once their desires have been defined, it becomes much easier to find solutions that will work. Here are some of the obstacles that they face, and ways to get over them.

Step 1. Freeze the estate

Freezing the estate involves reorganizing the share capital of the company and taking back two classes of voting preference shares for John's common shares. These shares are redeemable and retractable for $3.5 million, representing the current value of the firm.

Using a combination of planning techniques permitted under the Income Tax Act, John would take back two separate classes of preference shares. One class of shares would be redeemable for $500,000, and the second class would be redeemable for $3 million.

During this share reorganization, John would also increase the cost base of the first class of preference shares by $500,000, effectively creating a $500,000 capital gain. He would then claim the $500,000 capital gains exemption to offset this capital gain. Through this transaction, John has increased the cost base of his preferred shares by crystallizing the capital gains exemption. This will eliminate about $125,000 in taxes that would otherwise be due on the disposition of the preferred shares.

To realize the benefits of an estate freeze, new common shares are normally issued to the children who will take over the business in the future. All future growth will accrue to those common shares. So John effectively limits his tax liability to the current value of the business. He also locks in the capital gains exemption by utilizing it as part of this transaction. Of course, John needs to plan around the possible application of the alternative minimum tax, as discussed earlier.

Step 2. A little family trust

Since only one of John and Mary's children currently works with the company, and the couple wants to provide an opportunity for the other two children to come on board in the future (if that is what they want), they will also set up a family trust.

In this trust, the three adult children and any of John and Mary's grandchildren are discretionary beneficiaries. The couple and their accountant are the designated trustees and must act by majority decision.

The trust document expands the investment powers of the trustees to include owning shares in private corporations, as well as a number of other types of investments.

Once the trust is established, it will borrow $100 from John's bank. This money will be used to purchase new common voting shares in the firm. Any future growth in the value of the business will accrue to the benefit of these shares.

This arrangement allows John to keep control of the company. His preference shares can outvote the common shares, and he and Mary can effectively control the voting rights of the common shares as trustees of the family trust.

A family trust offers many benefits. First, the couple will have a number of years to figure out which child or children will receive shares in the company. As you may recall from Chapter 8, there is a deemed disposition of capital property in a family trust every 21 years. Lots of time to assess the situation.

Second, the transfer of the shares from the trust to the children can take place on a rollover basis, so no capital gains will be realized when the trust is wound up. Since Mary is also a beneficiary, the trust can transfer some or all of the common shares to her. This would come in handy if they wanted to unwind the estate freeze.

Why would they want to do that? The short answer is flexibility. John and Mary might want to share in the company's future increase in value. Or they may decide that they don't want the children getting shares in the company after all.

The family that stays together ...

A family trust also helps protect the business if one of the children gets into a messy divorce. By holding the shares in a discretionary trust, the spouse's entitlement to any value in the business should be fairly nominal. As well, shares in the company could not be transferred to the spouse in satisfaction of his or her family law entitlement, since the children do not directly own these shares.

A different kind of splitting

Under the rules in effect before 2000, the family trust could have been used as a vehicle to split income with minor children who are beneficiaries of the trust. The company would first pay dividends to the trust; the trust would then channel that income so that it would be taxed to the children.

The trust did this by using the dividend income to pay certain living expenses of the minor children. The trust would then deduct these payments in calculating its income. In turn, the minor children would include these payments in income as dividends for tax purposes. Assuming they had no other sources of income, the dividends would be subject to little or no tax.

But with the recent changes to the Income Tax Act (discussed in Chapter 4), income splitting opportunities with minor children are now limited.

However, capital gains splitting with minors can still be accomplished through a family trust. Moreover, the new rules do not affect children who have reached the age of 18. In John and Mary's case, then, it still makes sense to have the grandchildren as discretionary beneficiaries of the family trust.

A capital idea

A family trust can also minimize capital gains taxes on future growth. Let's say that the common shares owned by the family trust grow to be worth $2 million. And let's say it is determined that one of the kids is going to take over the business on John's retirement or earlier death. One option would be for the family trust to transfer the shares to this child. This would take place on a rollover basis, so no capital gain would be triggered.

Instead, John's son or daughter would realize the gain on a subsequent sale or upon death. The couple's will would be structured to make sure that the other two children would receive their fair share of the estate.

The trick is to multiply the use of the $500,000 capital gains exemption. Here's how that plan would play out. At the appropriate time, the family trust would distribute shares with $500,000 of accrued capital gains to those children who are not active in the business. The remainder of the shares would go to the active child or children. Prior to this transfer, the children would enter into a buy-sell agreement that would give the active child or children the right to purchase the shares—at their current fair market value—of the inactive children.

An interest-bearing promissory note would be given to the inactive children in respect of the sale price. Although those children would each realize a capital gain of $500,000 on the sale, they could offset it by using the capital gains exemption. The sale may have to be structured over several years to avoid the application of the alternative minimum tax.

Having the active child or children purchase the shares will increase their cost base. This will reduce the amount of capital gains arising from a subsequent disposition of the shares.

Coming up with the money

If we assume that only one child will be active in the business when John dies, here's how the plan should go.

The company should take out an insurance policy on John's life for, say, $1 million. Upon his death, the insurance would be paid to the company, creating a credit to the company's capital dividend account.

An agreement between the firm and the family trust would require that the company use the insurance proceeds to pay a tax-free capital dividend to the trust. The trust would in turn pay out this dividend to the active child as a tax-free distribution of capital.

He or she would then use the insurance proceeds to pay off the promissory notes to the other siblings. This would give them each $500,000 in cash and would leave the active child with control of the company.

The way of the will

John's and Mary's existing wills should be revised to make sure that they fit with the succession plan. In fact, they should each have two wills.

The first would govern all their property except for shares in the business and will likely require probate. The second would deal solely with the shares in the company and will not require probate. This will avoid the payment of substantial probate taxes on the value of the shares in the firm.

Let's take a look at what would happen if John predeceases Mary. Under his first will, all of his property will be transferred directly to Mary on a rollover basis. Under the second will, the preference shares in the business will be transferred to a spousal trust. Again, this transfer will take place on a rollover basis and no taxes will be triggered.

Upon Mary's death, the preference shares will be transferred to those children who are active in the business. They will be able to use Mary's remaining capital gains exemption to reduce the capital gain on the preference shares to approximately $2.5 million.

As further protection, John will purchase a joint second-to-die policy for $2 million to cover the tax liability on the preference shares. Any proceeds not required for taxes will be distributed to those children who are not active in the business for estate equalization purposes.

This policy is less expensive than a policy covering either John's or Mary's life, since it only pays out upon the second death. And that's when liquidity is needed for taxes and to equalize the estate between the various children.

But in the meantime ...

While all this is well and fine for succession planning, there is the little matter of retirement income to factor into the scheme.

John's preference shares are redeemable at his discretion. He can also build in entitlement to dividends on those shares.

So John and Mary will have the flexibility to pay themselves dividends, or redeem the preference shares to supplement RRSP income.

Redeeming those preference shares with no adjusted cost base while John is still alive will also reduce the capital gains tax bill that arises upon the death of the last surviving spouse.

Introducing buy-sell agreements

It is somewhat unusual to have a buy-sell agreement between family members. They are more frequently used when dealing with partners that are not related to each other—in accounting-speak, arm's length shareholders.

A buy-sell agreement usually specifies the circumstances under which a shareholder will be required to sell his or her shares to the other shareholders. It also stipulates the method of determining the selling price.

The most common triggering events for these types of buy-sell agreements are the death, disability, or retirement of one of the shareholders.

Not enough to shake on it

There are a number of different ways to structure a buy-sell agreement between arm's length shareholders that takes effect upon the death of a shareholder. And like everything else, it should be on paper. A gentlemen's agreement won't cut it if there's a dispute between shareholders and the deceased's estate.

Let's rework the previous situation and give John an arm's length partner to demonstrate.

Assume that John's partner, Karen, owns 40 percent of the shares of the company. If the business is worth $3.5 million, John's shares are worth $2.1 million while Karen's are worth $1.4 million. The partners want to enter into a buy-sell agreement that governs the purchase and sale of their shares upon the death of either shareholder.

One method of structuring the agreement is known as the criss-cross buy-sell. Under this arrangement, the surviving shareholder is required to purchase the deceased's shares from his or her estate.

Assuming John dies first, he will be deemed to have disposed of his shares at fair market value. His final tax return will show a taxable capital gain of about $550,000 (50 percent of the $2.1 million value less the $500,000 cost base resulting from the crystallization of the capital gains exemption).

His partner will pay $2.1 million for the shares. Assuming the shares were all of the same class, this would increase the cost base of all her shares by $2.1 million.

Under most buy-sell agreements that take effect upon death, the purchase price is usually funded with life insurance. John would own and pay the premiums on a policy for $1.4 million on the life of his partner. She, in turn, would own and pay the premiums on a $2.1 million policy on his life.

Not without problems
While this is probably the simplest way to structure and fund a buy-sell agreement, a number of problems can arise. First of all, Karen may have cash flow problems in respect to the insurance policy—she is buying a larger policy on the life of an elderly individual.

There may also be a concern about keeping the coverage in force. If one shareholder fails to pay the premiums, the required funds may not be available to purchase the deceased's shares.

To redeem or not to redeem, that is the question
As a result of these concerns, structuring the buy-sell agreement as a corporate share redemption may be preferable. Under this type of arrangement, the company would be required to redeem the deceased's shares, using the proceeds of a corporate-owned insurance policy. This will allow all the shareholders to confirm that the company is maintaining the policies' premiums.

It will also be more cost-effective for the company to own the policies, especially if the company is in a lower tax bracket than the shareholders. This is because the premium must be funded with after-tax dollars. The criss-cross method can also work well in this situation.

When the company owns the policies, the shareholders indirectly split costs in proportion to their share ownership. This minimizes inequities that can result from one shareholder being older or in a higher risk category.

And now, the cost

No matter how well you plan things, there always seems to be one more issue that makes life a bit more difficult. Usually, that's the tax consequences.

In recent years, things have become more complicated due to the stop-loss rules and other provisions applicable to corporate-owned insurance.

With the situation we've been describing, John's death will result in the deemed disposition of his shares at fair market value. This will result in a taxable capital gain of approximately $500,000 on his final tax return.

The next step is the redemption of the shares by his estate. Proceeds received by the estate will be treated as a dividend to the extent that the redemption price exceeds the paid-up capital of the shares. Paid-up capital is a corporate law term that normally represents the initial amount paid for the shares by the original subscriber.

In most cases this is a very nominal amount. What this means is that most of the redemption proceeds will be taxed as a dividend. However, there is a mechanism whereby this dividend can be received tax-free by the estate.

This comes from the special tax treatment provided to insurance proceeds that are received by a private corporation. The difference between the death benefit and the policy's adjusted cost basis creates a credit to the company's capital dividend account.

The capital dividend account consists of amounts that would be tax-free if paid directly to the shareholder, including insurance proceeds. A company can pay dividends out of the capital dividend account on a tax-free basis.

Still not out of the woods yet

The buy-sell agreement will require the company to elect that any dividend arising from the redemption of shares upon death will be treated as a capital dividend. Consequently, John's estate would pay no tax on the redemption of the shares.

This is where things can get a bit tricky. For tax purposes, the redemption of the shares is treated as a disposition of those shares. However, the proceeds are reduced by the amount of the deemed dividend on the redemption. This is to eliminate the potential for double taxation.

In this case, the proceeds will be reduced to almost nil, since almost all of the $2.1 million received by the estate is treated as a dividend. This, in turn, creates a capital loss, since the estate inherited the shares with a cost base equal to the deemed proceeds upon death of $2.1 million.

Before the introduction of the stop-loss rules, this loss could be carried back to the final tax return of the deceased to offset the capital gain arising on the shares.

Unfortunately, the Department of Finance introduced rules effective as of April 26, 1995, that initially only allowed 25 percent of the capital loss to be carried back.

As a result of the October 2000 federal mini-budget (which reduced the capital gains inclusion rate to 50 percent), the Department of Finance has indicated that the Income Tax Act will be amended to allow 50 percent of the capital loss to be carried back. These tax provisions are referred to as the stop-loss rules.

Better than nothing

Despite these changes, in John's case the buy-sell agreement is still a good deal. This transaction will eliminate 50 percent of the gain that would otherwise be realized upon his death.

However, this ignores Karen's tax position as the surviving shareholder. The redemption of his shares with the life insurance proceeds means that Karen's shares are now worth $3.5 million. But since she did not directly pay anything to John's estate in respect to his shares, Karen does not benefit from a higher cost base. This means that she will realize a $3.5 million gain when she disposes of her shares in the company.

There is an element of double taxation here, since John's estate has already paid tax on 50 percent of the gain attributable to his shares.

But just as there are a number of tax rules to add revenue to the government's coffers, there are also a number of planning strategies that can be used to minimize the impact of the stop-loss rules and maximize the benefits of corporate-owned insurance.

What you should know is that the stop-loss rules do have an impact on buy-sell planning. There are also grandfathering rules for life insurance that were put in place before April 27, 1995, for corporate share redemption, as well as for shares subject to a buy-sell agreement in place prior to that date.

Aside from stop-loss rules, there are also some other potential problems associated with corporate-owned insurance.

- The insurance cash values and death benefit are subject to attachment by the company's creditors.
- Problems can arise if the shareholders sell the company to a third party but want to retain the insurance for personal purposes—the transfer of the policy may result in tax exposure for both the company and shareholders.

- Cash values of a permanent insurance policy may have an impact on the entitlement to the $500,000 capital gains exemption, since the policy is not considered an active business asset.

These issues can usually be dealt with by placing the insurance policies with a holding company. The operating company can pay dividends to the holding company on a tax-free basis to fund the premiums. This insulates the policy from the operating company's creditors and allows the operating company to be sold while retaining control of the insurance policies. If properly structured, the use of a holding company to own the insurance policies may also allow the shares of the operating company to continue to qualify for the capital gains exemption.

IN THE NEXT CHAPTER
- Why you need outside expertise
- Looking for the right help
- What a planner should offer you
- What you can expect to pay

11

The money is under the mattress. So now what do I do?

You now know a little more about planning your estate. The next step is finding the person to make it happen

IT'S HARD TO MAKE PREDICTIONS,
ESPECIALLY ABOUT THE FUTURE.
—Lawrence Peter "Yogi" Berra

Some people are content to keep their money in a shoebox on the top shelf of a closet or under their bed. Some have the foresight to amass a well-balanced portfolio of investments, including stocks, bonds, GICs, and mutual funds.

Whatever approach you choose, you still have to figure out what to do with your wealth as time marches on. Of course, some funds will be used to finance your retirement. But after you pass on, whatever is left will go to your loved ones. An estate plan is essential.

Even those of you who are inclined to overspend—and figure that you'll blow your estate, including the children's inheritances, by the time you expire—can benefit greatly from an estate plan. As you may have gleaned from the previous chapters, an estate plan does more than just deal with your assets after death. It can also help you hold onto or increase your wealth, providing a better lifestyle in your golden years.

Your estate plan is insurance for you and for your family's future. And since it's pretty hard to figure out everything that's going to happen down the road, you have to have strategies in place to handle a whole range of possibilities.

Best left to experts

"It's not over 'til it's over" is another celebration of the obvious attributed to Yogi Berra. True as this may be, the big problem is that no matter your age, you never know when it's going to be over. You need to be prepared.

And like every other complicated aspect of modern life—debugging your computer, interpreting Canada's tax laws, programming your VCR—it's best to leave it to the experts.

Finding that expert can be a challenge. The first wall to climb over is that of your own misgivings—just like when you place your savings and investments under the auspices of a financial adviser. It's hard to do, handing over such a personal and valuable aspect of your life.

The same goes for an estate planner. And, as you've learned, there's a lot of personal and confidential information that has to be shared, at least initially, with a stranger.

For those who already have a financial adviser or planner, that person (or others in the company) may well have the expertise to look after your estate. This could be a good route to take. Your adviser should already know most of your financial details, and hopefully you've developed a good working relationship.

But many Canadians don't have a formal financial plan or a trusted adviser to whom they can turn to with their estate planning concerns.

Finding the comfort zone

There's no real set of rules to follow when trying to find an individual with the expertise to handle your estate planning needs. Depending on what's involved and the related sensitivities, the estate planning experience can be very intense.

You may have spent many years accumulating wealth and possessions, and often these possessions—a family business, a cottage, family heirlooms—have special meaning. In many cases, they are the only tangible reminders of life's sacrifices, hard efforts, and family heritage.

In determining what happens to these possessions, you are confronting your own retirement and eventual demise. This process can release significant emotions, making it difficult to face up to the necessary decisions.

Seek, and you shall find

You may already have a good working relationship with some key advisers—your lawyer, investment planner, accountant, or banker. Each one has used his or her particular skills to assist you in various situations, and each may have a fair amount of knowledge on the estate planning front. However, your best bet will be to find someone who can pull together a comprehensive plan—one that integrates the areas handled by all of these individuals, and addresses both your needs and those of your children.

How do you find such a person? Use common sense. When you're looking for a renovation contractor, a financial adviser, or even a nanny, you ask a friend, relative, or colleague if they know of someone who can get the job done.

That's a great place to start, especially if that acquaintance has had a good experience using the services of the referred individual. But even with a referral, it's still a good idea to ask your potential estate planner for the names of three of his or her clients who would be willing to provide references. A good estate planner should be happy to accommodate this request. If you are able to ascertain that this individual is highly respected and effective, you have started off on the right foot.

The big three

As important as it is to have someone who comes highly recommended, it is equally important to ask a lot of questions—questions about experience and qualifications, professional degrees, and planning philosophies. Based on what you've read here, you should make notes regarding the areas you want to discuss. You should also have the information that your planner will need ready and available. That means having at least a rough idea of what you'd like to accomplish. If you're not sure about this, a good planner will be able to help you sketch out what is required, based on his or her experience.

Any planner that you are assessing should have three major strengths.

Knowledge
Their area of expertise should include:
- will planning
- investment and retirement planning
- tax planning
- family law
- trusts
- insurance strategies and products
- charitable giving
- taxation upon death

Experience

A planner's proven track record should include:
- 5 to 10 years of experience in estate planning
- solid references
- sound reputation in the professional community

Professional designations/affiliations

Other aspects of a planner's profile could include:
- Bachelor of Laws (LL.B.), Chartered Accountant (C.A.), Chartered Financial Planner, Chartered Life Underwriter
- membership in an estate planning organization
- articles published in recognized industry journals
- public speaking on estate planning subjects

Even with these strengths in place, do not be lulled into believing that you found the perfect candidate. You also need to assess how your candidate interacts with you. Do you connect? And ask yourself if that person can work co-operatively with the other professional people in your life—your lawyer, financial adviser, or accountant.

Also, the potential candidate should provide some literature outlining his or her services, as well as some of the key issues in drawing up your estate.

It all comes down to money

Many individuals are hesitant to initiate a financial or estate plan, believing that it's going to cost an arm and a leg. That couldn't be further from the truth.

On the financial planning side of things, many advisers do not charge for their services—they are compensated if you purchase certain products from various financial institutions.

In simple words, they work on commission. It's the same as buying a plane ticket from a travel agent. The airline returns part of your payment to the agent for their services. You pay the same regardless of whether you buy directly from the airline or from the agent.

Estate planners are usually compensated in the same way. They receive commissions or other payments if you purchase insurance products, investment vehicles, or related products needed to implement the plan.

You will usually be responsible for any legal or accounting fees. If needed, your planner can assist you in selecting experienced professionals in these areas.

By all means, ask your potential planner what costs are involved. With trusts and other legal documents like wills and powers of attorney, there will be legal costs. A good planner will itemize any anticipated costs so that you know ahead of time what will be required.

Not a one-time proposition

Preparing an estate plan is a great way to achieve some peace of mind in today's whirlwind world. It provides a little stability as things continue to change with increasing speed.

Because of the way things change, you have to ensure that your estate planner is capable of adapting your plan to keep it current. A great deal of this responsibility lies with you. You have to ensure that he or she is informed when circumstances change; for example, the arrival of a child or grandchild, family deaths, separation or divorce, changes in financial status, real estate disposition, and the like.

However, an experienced estate planner will usually prompt you to disclose changes in your family's circumstances through ongoing follow-ups. And this maintenance service should be as important a consideration as the initial planning process.

Be prepared to find out how often your planner will provide a checkup—at least yearly makes sense. Does he or she send out a regular newsletter or other relevant literature, or does he or she stage seminars that might be of interest?

Worth the effort

What it all boils down to is this: for a relatively minimal cost, a little bit of your time, and a firm commitment to add some structure to your circumstances, you can easily prepare yourself and your family for the vagaries and stresses of modern living.

You can't entirely eliminate all the unknowns. But by minimizing most of them and having an action plan in place, you can significantly reduce worry, stress, and even fear. After all, drawing up an estate plan is *not* a surrender to mortality—it's a commitment to a better quality of life.

Appendix
Estate Planning Factfinder*

PERSONAL DATA

Date: _____

Client

Name: _____ Date of Birth: _____ Sex: ☐ Male ☐ Female

Home Address: _____

Telephone: Res: _____ Bus: _____ Fax: _____

Email: _____ Smoker: ☐ Yes ☐ No

Are you a Canadian Resident?   ☐ Yes   ☐ No

Occupation: _____

Business Address: _____

Are you married?   ☐ Yes   ☐ No

Where were you married? _____ When? _____

Is there a marriage contract?   ☐ Yes   ☐ No

Have you been married previously?   ☐ Yes   ☐ No

   If yes, any support obligations?   ☐ Yes   ☐ No   Amount: _____

Spouse

Name: _____ Date of Birth: _____ Sex: ☐ Male ☐ Female

Home Address: _____

Telephone: Res: _____ Bus: _____ Fax: _____

Email: _____ Smoker: ☐ Yes ☐ No

Canadian Resident?   ☐ Yes   ☐ No

Occupation: _____

Business Address: _____

*To obtain additional copies of the Estate Planning Factfinder, or to complete online, visit
www.equinoxfinancial.ca, highlight "Benefit" and select "Estate Planning."

185

CHILDREN

Name	Sex	Married/ Single	Date of Birth/Age	Comments (Please indicate residency if other than Canadian)

GRANDCHILDREN

Parents Name	Name	Sex	Date of Birth/Age	Comments (Please indicate residency if other than Canadian)

Are any of your children/grandchildren adopted?   ☐ Yes   ☐ No

   Is adoption complete?   ☐ Yes   ☐ No

Name: _____

Do you have any other dependents?   ☐ Yes   ☐ No

Name: _____

Do any of your children/grandchildren have special needs?   ☐ Yes   ☐ No

Please describe: _____

LIQUID ASSETS

	Description/ Comments/ Purchase Date	Client	Spouse	Jointly	ACB/UCC
		Current Fair Market Value			
Bank Accounts	_____	_____	_____	_____	
Bonds (other than private company)	_____	_____	_____	_____	_____
Stock Portfolio	_____	_____	_____	_____	_____
Savings Plans or Certificates	_____	_____	_____	_____	
Mutual Funds	_____	_____	_____	_____	_____
Segregated Funds	_____	_____	_____	_____	_____
Notes Receivable	_____	_____	_____	_____	
Life Insurance, Cash Values	_____	_____	_____	_____	
RRSPs	_____	_____	_____	_____	
Commutable Annuities, RRIFs	_____	_____	_____	_____	
Other	_____	_____	_____	_____	_____
TOTAL LIQUID ASSETS		════════	════════	════════	

NON-LIQUID ASSETS

	Description/ Comments/ Purchase Date	Client	Spouse	Jointly	ACB/UCC
		Current Fair Market Value			
Residence	_____	_____	_____	_____	_____
Cottage	_____	_____	_____	_____	_____
Other Real Estate	_____	_____	_____	_____	_____
Business Interests	_____	_____	_____	_____	_____
Personal and Household Effects	_____	_____	_____	_____	_____
Automobiles, Boats, etc.	_____	_____	_____	_____	_____
Notes from Family Members	_____	_____	_____	_____	_____
Collectors Items	_____	_____	_____	_____	_____
Mortgages	_____	_____	_____	_____	_____
Non-Commutable Annuities	_____	_____	_____	_____	
DPSP, RPP	_____	_____	_____	_____	
Other Non-Liquid Assets	_____	_____	_____	_____	_____
TOTAL NON-LIQUID ASSETS		_____	_____	_____	

LIABILITIES

	Description/Comments	Client	Spouse	Jointly
Bank Loans (Life Insured ☐ Yes ☐ No)				
Life Insurance Policy Loans				
Mortgages (Indicate property concerned)				
Credit Cards				
Loans from Family Members				
Other Indebtedness				
TOTAL LIABILITIES				
Net Worth (Total Assets - Total Liabilities)				

Additional Notes _____

CURRENT SOURCES OF INCOME

	Description/Comments	Client	Spouse	Jointly
Employment				
Dividends				
Interest				
Rent				
Annuities				
RRSPs/RRIFs				
Pension Plans				
CPP/QPP/OAS				
Other				
TOTAL INCOME				

ESTATE DISTRIBUTION

Do you have a will? ☐ Yes ☐ No

Who prepared your will? _____

Last reviewed (Date) _____

Does your spouse have a will? ☐ Yes ☐ No

Who prepared your spouse's will? _____

Last reviewed (Date) _____

Have you appointed a guardian for minor children? ☐ Yes ☐ No ☐ N/A

Name and address of guardian: _____

Who is/are the executor(s) of your will? Name: _____

_____

_____

Is your executor knowledgeable about:

Your family's needs? ☐ Yes ☐ No
Investments ? ☐ Yes ☐ No
Running a business? ☐ Yes ☐ No
Tax and Trust laws? ☐ Yes ☐ No

Where do you keep your will? _____

Can I get a copy of you and your spouse's will? ☐ Yes ☐ No

Do you have a power of attorney? ☐ Yes ☐ No
　　Your Spouse? ☐ Yes ☐ No

Do you have a power of attorney for personal care (living will?) ☐ Yes ☐ No

Who prepared your power of attorney? _____

Last reviewed? (Date) _____

Can I get a copy of your and your spouse's power of attorney? ☐ Yes ☐ No

WILL PLANNING

(If no current will or will needs revision)

On you predeceasing your spouse:

How much income will your spouse/
family require to maintain his/her/
their standard of living? $_____

Do you want this income indexed?   ☐ Yes   ☐ No

   If Yes, at what rate?   _____

What is a reasonable rate of interest that
could be earned on invested capital? $_____

Specific bequests at death: ☐ Yes   What property: _____

                                             _____

                                             _____

                                             ☐ No   To whom: _____

                                             ☐ Other _____

                                             (explain) _____

Disposition of residue (other than
business interests)   _____

☐ Bequests to children $_____ Or _____% At age _____

☐ Immediate to spouse $_____ Or _____% Absolutely

☐ In trust solely for benefit of spouse   Explain: _____

☐ In trust with income only to spouse   _____ With capital to children at
                                             spouse's death_____

☐ Other distributions as follows: _____

Disposition of business interests: _____

☐ To be liquidated and included as   Estimated liquidation value $ _____
  part of residue

☐ Business to be retained?   ☐ Yes   ☐ No

  Who will continue the business?   _____

  Who will receive the business?   _____

OTHER

Where do you keep your life insurance policies?

_____

At which banks do you maintain your accounts?

_____

Do you have a safety deposit box? ☐ Yes ☐ No

If Yes, where? _____

Who is your Accountant?

Name: _____

Firm: _____

Phone #: _____

Who is your Lawyer?

Name: _____

Firm: _____

Phone #: _____

Who is your Investment Advisor?

Name: _____

Firm: _____

Phone #: _____

May I have the permission to consult any of these advisors if necessary? ☐ Yes ☐ No

May I have the permission to consult any life insurance companies regarding your present insurance? ☐ Yes ☐ No

Do you anticipate receiving any gifts or inheritances? ☐ Yes ☐ No

From Whom? _____

When? _____

Approximate amount? $_____

BUSINESS INTERESTS

Is this business operated as a: ☐ Sole Proprietorship
☐ Partnership
☐ Incorporated Company (fiscal year end _____)

When was the business formed or incorporated? _____

Firm Name: _____

Description of business: _____

Partner/Shareholder	Address	Age	Sex	Smoking Status	How Active

	Common	Preferred
Number of issued shares	_____	_____
Number of shares held by you	_____	_____

Number of shares held by others:

_____ _____ _____

_____ _____ _____

_____ _____ _____

What is the total fair market value of the business? $ _____

What was the approximate value of your business on the later of
V-Day (December 1971) and the day you acquired your interest? $ _____

Can I obtain a copy of your financial statements for the last 3 years? ☐ Yes ☐ No

Does your firm have any individuals whose contributions seriously
affect the profits of the business? ☐ Yes ☐ No

If Yes, who? _____

Name	Age	Smoker	Position	Salary

What group benefits does your firm provide?

☐ Group Life   ☐ Weekly Income   ☐ L.T.D.   ☐ Major Medical
☐ Dental   ☐ Pension Plan   ☐ Other

Are there different benefit levels for various employee classes? ☐ Yes ☐ No

Does your firm have a: ☐ Deferred Profit Sharing Plan ☐ Group RRSP
☐ Non-Registered Pension Plan ☐ Retirement Comp. Arrangement

Number of employees in the company: _____

BUSINESS CONTINUATION

Do you have a buy-sell agreement?   ☐ Yes ☐ No

   If Yes, can I get a copy of your buy-sell agreement?   ☐ Yes ☐ No

   If No, are there any succession plans in place?   ☐ Yes ☐ No

   If Yes, please describe: _____

   If Yes, how is the price determined in the agreement? _____

   Is this agreement fully funded with life insurance?   ☐ Yes ☐ No

What arrangements have you made for the continuation of your business operation in the event of your retirement or disability?

_____

If business is a partnership:

Name: _____ Capital Amount: _____

Name: _____ Capital Amount: _____

Name: _____ Capital Amount: _____

If business is incorporated:

Does the corporation qualify for the small business deduction?   ☐ Yes ☐ No

Do the shares qualify for the enhanced capital gains exemption? ☐ Yes ☐ No

   Amount of exemption claimed by client? $_____

What is the balance of your cumulative net investment losses? $_____

What is the balance of the RDTOH account? $_____

What is the balance of the capital dividend account? $_____

Estimated Annual Growth rate of company   _____%

STRUCTURE OF OWNERSHIP

Use this page to create a schematic showing all business owners and their respective interests. You should also indicate whether there are holding companies and/or multiple operating companies.

LIFE INSURANCE AND GROUP PLANS

(include business coverage and group life)

	Company	Plan	Face Amount	Riders	Cash Value	Owner	Beneficiary	Premium
On Self								
On Business Associates								
On Spouse's Life								
On Children								

Has any insurance been purchased for collateral purposes? ☐ Yes ☐ No   Please indicate with an *

	Company	Plan	Face Amount	Riders	Cash Value	Owner	Beneficiary	Premium
Disability Insurance								
Pensions, DPSP, RRSP								
Critical Illness Insurance								
Long Term Care								

REGISTERED INVESTMENTS

Fixed Income:

Issuer	Original Deposit	Current Value	Interest Rate	Maturity Date	Spousal	Beneficiary

Equity Based:

Issuer	Original Deposit	Current Value	Current # of Units	Current Unit Value	Spousal	Beneficiary

RETIREMENT PLANS

When do you plan to retire? Age: _____

What level of income will you require? $ _____

Do you want this income indexed for inflation? ☐ Yes ☐ No

If Yes, at what rate?_____%

How much income will your spouse require if you predecease him/her? $ _____

Sources/Amounts of Retirement Income RRSPs $ _____

Pension Plans $ _____

Government Benefits $ _____

Non-Registered Funds $ _____

NON-REGISTERED INVESTMENTS

Fixed Income:

Issuer	Original Deposit	Current Value	Interest Rate	Maturity Date	Beneficiary

Equity Based:

Issuer	Original Deposit	Current Value	Current # of Units	Maturity Date	Beneficiary

Estate Planning Objectives

FINANCIAL   **Rating**
                                      (1 = highest, 15 = lowest)

1. Maximizing Retirement Income   _____
2. Maximizing Estate Values   _____
3. Minimizing Probate Fees   _____
4. Minimizing taxes while alive   _____
5. Minimizing taxes to beneficiaries   _____

FAMILY

1. Providing income to spouse and dependents   _____
2. Updating/completing wills   _____
3. Updating/completing Powers of Attorney   _____
4. Establishing a family trust   _____
5. Funding costs related to illness or hospitalization   _____

DISPOSITION OF ESTATE

1. Establishing trusts for dependent children/grandchildren   _____
2. Making a gift to charities   _____
3. Appointing guardians for minor children   _____
4. Successful transfer to business interests   _____
5. Taking care of special need dependents   _____

NOTES

NOTES

Glossary

A

active business—generally any activity carried on by a corporation (other than certain investment or personal service businesses). A business must be active to qualify for certain tax preferences, including the capital gains exemption and small business deduction.

actuary—an insurance professional that prices insurance products using mathematical assumptions concerning mortality, investment returns, and administrative expenses.

adjusted cost base—the cost of property for tax purposes. If capital property is sold, the capital gain or loss is measured as the difference between the selling price and the property's adjusted cost base.

administrator—an individual that is appointed by the court to manage the estate of someone who has not appointed an executor under his or her will.

alter ego trust—a trust established by a settlor who is 65 years of age or older. It is for the settlor's exclusive benefit during his or her lifetime. The trust provides that no person other than the settlor can have any absolute or contingent interest as beneficiary under the trust while the settlor is alive.

alternative minimum tax (AMT)—a separate tax regime under the Income Tax Act to ensure that all taxpayers pay their fair portion of taxes. In particular, certain deductions that are otherwise tax free (i.e., the tax-free portion of capital gains) or tax deductible are added back into income.

annuitant—the person who holds or receives an annuity. Under a life annuity, the annuitant receives payments for as long as he or she is alive.

annuity—an insurance product whereby the owner makes payments to the insurance company in return for a guaranteed income over a pre-set time.

appreciated assets—assets that have grown in value over time and will likely result in a capital gain when sold.

arm's length—where two parties are not related by blood or other personal or business relationships. Relevant for determining the tax consequences of transactions between parties.

B

beneficiary—the person designated by a settlor, testator, or testatrix as being entitled to income and/or capital under a trust or estate.

buy-sell agreement—an agreement between business owners that sets the terms for buying out an owner's interest in a business under certain circumstances (such as death or disability).

C

Canadian-controlled private corporation—a private corporation that is controlled by Canadians, not non-residents.

Canadian Education Savings Grant (CESG)—a grant provided by the federal government to bolster contributions to a Registered Education Savings Plan. The maximum federal grant is 20% of the annual contribution up to a maximum of $400 per year for each child.

capital dividend account—a special tax account for private corporations that reflects the receipt of certain tax-free amounts such as life insurance proceeds. A corporation can pay tax-free dividends out of its capital dividend account.

capital gain—the value of a capital property's growth from the time it was acquired to when it was sold or otherwise disposed of. Currently, 50 percent of the capital gain is taxable.

capital gains crystallization—a transaction that permits a taxpayer to lock in the capital gains exemption, in respect to shares in a private corporation, by increasing the cost base of the shares.

capital loss—the loss in value of a capital property from the time it was acquired to when it was sold. Currently, 50 percent of a capital loss can be claimed as a deduction against capital gains.

claw back—eligibility for certain government benefits such as Old Age Security is based on a recipient's income. If a recipient's income exceeds a certain level, the benefit is subject to a special tax, or "claw back."

codicil—an amendment or addition to a will that is signed by a testator or testatrix and witnessed using the same formalities that apply to a will.

common shares—a type of corporate share that yields flexible dividends (at the discretion of the board of directors) and entitles shareholders to benefit from future business growth.

criss-cross buy-sell—a form of buy-sell agreement where a shareholder is required to buy the other shareholder's interest upon death. Each shareholder usually owns insurance on the other shareholder's life to fund the buyout.

D

deemed sale—the Income Tax Act contains provisions that treat an individual as having disposed of property for tax purposes even though ownership is retained. The most common situation arises upon death, where the deceased is deemed to have sold all capital property at fair market value immediately before death unless the property passes to a surviving spouse.

defined benefit plan—an employer-sponsored pension plan where the benefit amount reflects a percentage of an employee's earnings in conjunction with years of service with the employer.

defined contribution plan—an employer-sponsored pension plan where the benefit amount depends on the contributions made to the plan and investment returns.

depreciable capital property—a type of capital property whose value normally declines over time (i.e. machinery or vehicles). If the property is used for business purposes, the reduction in value can be claimed as an expense under the Income Tax Act.

directors' fees—most presidents and officers of incorporated businesses are accountable to a board of directors. A fee is paid to those directors for their services.

discretionary trust—a type of trust (either inter vivos or testamentary) where the trustee has the discretion to allocate income and capital among the beneficiaries.

disposition of assets—the sale or transfer of assets that will have tax consequences for the owner.

diversification—investing in different types of stocks and mutual funds to reduce the risk of loss.

dividend income—the distribution of profits from a corporation to its shareholders. Dividend income is entitled to preferential tax treatment since it has already been taxed at the corporate level.

E

earned income—certain types of income—including salary, wages, partnership income, and alimony payments—that allow an individual to make an RRSP contribution.

election—a right or entitlement provided under the Income Tax Act.

enduring power of attorney—a power of attorney that continues to be effective even after the mental incapacity of the donor.

equalization claim—a right under the Ontario Family Law Act that allows one spouse to make a claim against the property of another spouse upon death or the breakdown of their marriage.

equity investment—a type of investment (i.e., mutual funds or shares) where the underlying value is based on the financial circumstances of an incorporated business.

estate freeze—a transaction that allows a business owner to exchange shares that are escalating in value for shares and other assets that are fixed in value. An estate freeze is undertaken to limit the shareholder's future capital gains liability.

estate taxes—taxes imposed on assets owned at the time of death. While Canada does not impose estate taxes, Canadian residents can be subject to U.S. estate taxes if they own certain properties in the U.S.

executor—a person appointed by a testator or testatrix to administer the terms and conditions of his or her will. Also known as an estate trustee.

exempt insurance policy—a special type of life insurance policy under which the cash values can accumulate on a tax-deferred basis and be received tax-free upon death.

F

fair market value—generally the price that would be determined by a willing vendor in possession of all relevant facts. The Income Tax Act specifies that certain dispositions take place at "fair market value," including those between parties not dealing at arm's length.

family trust—an inter vivos trust established by a parent or grandparent for other family members to reduce income taxes and transfer property upon death.

fiduciary duty—the duty of a trustee to act in the best interests of the trust beneficiaries.

G

general anti-avoidance rules—rules contained in the Income Tax Act to prevent taxpayers from unduly avoiding, reducing, or deferring tax.

gifting—the transfer of property from one person to another without consideration. Gifts of property are normally made by parents to children for estate planning purposes.

guaranteed investment certificate (GIC)—an investment offered by a bank or trust company that guarantees the return of the original investment plus a specified amount of interest.

guardian—a person appointed in a will or by the court to assume responsibility for minor children as a result of their parents' death or disability.

H

holding company—an inactive company interposed between individual shareholders and an operating company for tax and estate planning purposes.

I

income attribution rules—rules established under the Income Tax Act to discourage spouses and parents from shifting income-earning property between family members to reduce the overall tax burden on the income earned from the property.

income splitting—the transfer of income-producing properties to family members in a lower tax bracket to reduce the overall amount of tax payable on the income.

inter vivos trust—a trust established while the settlor is alive. An inter vivos trust is considered a separate taxpayer, subject to tax at the highest marginal rate applicable to individuals.

intestate—a situation that arises when a person dies without a valid will. Each province has rules governing the distribution of a person's estate if this occurs.

in-trust account—an investment account established by a parent for the benefit of minor children. The investments normally consist of equity mutual funds or stocks to take advantage of certain exceptions to the income attribution rules.

irrevocable beneficiary—a beneficiary under an insurance policy whose entitlement to benefits cannot be changed without his or her consent.

J

joint partner trust—a trust created after 1999 by a settlor who is 65 or older. It is for the exclusive benefit of the settlor and his or her spouse (which includes a common-law spouse or same-sex partner) during their joint lives. The trust provides that no person other than the settlor and his or her spouse can have any absolute or contingent interest as beneficiary under the trust while the settlor or spouse is alive.

joint tenancy—a form of ownership where the co-owners have equal, undivided interests in a property. Upon the death of one joint tenant, the other co-owner assumes total ownership of the property without the deceased's interest passing through his or her estate.

L

Life Income Fund (LIF)—a financial planning option available to those individuals transferring from a pension plan or locked-in RRSP.

liquid assets—assets (such as term deposits or guaranteed investment certificates) that consist of cash or can easily be converted to cash.

living will—a legal document that allows a person to indicate his or her wishes regarding future medical treatment if that person is unable to give consent due to incapacity.

Locked-in Retirement Account (LIRA)—A type of RRSP that accepts funds from a pension plan. The funds are subject to certain restrictions specified by provincial pension legislation, including limitations on early withdrawals and the type of maturity options.

Locked-in Retirement Income Fund (LRIF)—A type of RRIF that accepts funds from a locked-in RRSP or LIRA. Unlike a regular RRIF, there are restrictions on the maximum annual payouts from an LRIF.

locking-in restrictions—restrictions imposed by provincial pension legislation on funds transferred out from an employer-sponsored pension plan.

M

marginal tax rate—as individual taxpayers earn more income, they pay tax at higher rates on additional income. The highest rate of tax being imposed is known as the taxpayer's marginal tax rate.

marital tax credit—a credit available to offset U.S. estate taxes if U.S situs property is gifted to the surviving spouse.

N

net family property—under the Ontario Family Law Act, the value of specific property acquired by spouses during their marriage. The difference between the respective spouses' net family property is subject to division upon the breakdown of their marriage or death.

nominal adjusted cost base—where the adjusted cost base of a property is nil or close to nil.

non-recourse loan or financing—a form of debt or loan. If the borrower defaults, the lender can only pursue repayment by liquidating property acquired by the borrower with the loaned funds.

non-registered assets—investment assets held outside an RESP, RRSP, RRIF, or pension plan.

notary public—an individual authorized by the province to witness affidavits and other legal documents.

P

partnership—a non-incorporated business enterprise where the co-owners agree to share the profits and losses of the business in preset percentages.

pension maximization—a decision by the recipient of pension income to receive pension benefits that cease upon his or her death. Life insurance is acquired or maintained to provide capital and income to the surviving spouse.

permanent insurance—a type of life insurance that is designed to remain in force over an extended period of time. A higher premium is charged to subsidize insurance costs in the future.

power of attorney—a document that gives legal authority for one person to act in another's place.

preference shares—a type of corporate share that entitles the owner to dividends in preference to common shareholders and a preferential return of capital upon the dissolution of the company.

prenuptial contract—a contract entered into prior to marriage that governs entitlement to property in the event of divorce.

prescribed annuity—a certain type of payout annuity whose income is entitled to preferential tax treatment.

private corporation—a corporation that is not controlled by a public company and may have restrictions on the total number of shareholders. (Also see Canadian-controlled private corporation.)

private foundations—a type of foundation that does not qualify as a public foundation because one donor has contributed most of the capital or the directors and trustees are related to each other.

probate—a court declaration that the deceased's will is valid and third parties can deal with the appointed executor.

prospectus—a disclosure document prepared by a corporation or a mutual fund company and approved by provincial securities regulators in order to issue shares or units to the public.

public company—a company whose shares are approved for trading on a recognized stock exchange.

publicly traded shares—shares of a public company that are available to investors through a recognized stock exchange.

Public Trustee—a person or office appointed under provincial law to ensure the proper administration of estates and trusts, and protect the interests of minors.

R

recapture—taxable income arising from the disposition of depreciable property. It represents a recovery of deductable expenses previously claimed in respect of that property.

Registered Education Savings Plan (RESP)—a plan that meets certain conditions under the Income Tax Act and is established to accumulate funds for post-secondary education. Contributions are eligible for the Canadian Education Savings Grant, and accumulated income is tax deferred.

Registered Pension Plan (RPP)—a plan that meets certain conditions under the Income Tax Act and provincial pension legislation, and is established by an employer to accumulate funds on a tax-deferred basis for an employee's retirement.

Registered Retirement Income Fund (RRIF)—a plan that meets certain conditions under the Income Tax Act and is established to pay out retirement funds from an RRSP.

Registered Retirement Savings Plan (RRSP)—a plan that meets certain conditions under the Income Tax Act and is established by an individual to accumulate funds on a tax-deferred basis for retirement.

residue—the assets that remain in a person's estate after the payment of debts, expenses, and bequests.

reverse mortgage—a program under which an individual borrows funds based on the security of his or her home equity for retirement purposes. No loan repayments (including interest) are required until the home is sold or until the death of the borrower.

rollover—the transfer of property, usually between spouses or other related parties, at its adjusted cost base. This defers any capital gains until a subsequent sale or disposition of the property.

RRSP carry forward—refers to the portion of the RRSP deduction that is not utilized in one year, and can be carried forward and used in future tax years.

S

second-to-die life insurance—a life insurance policy where two people are insured and the insurance proceeds are only payable upon the death of the second life insured. This type of policy is normally used by spouses to cover capital gains tax liabilities arising upon the second death.

settlor—a person who establishes an inter vivos trust by specifying the beneficiaries, setting out the trust provisions, and transferring property to the trustees to hold for the benefit of the beneficiaries.

situs property—refers to property owned in the U.S.—real estate, bank accounts, shares—by Canadians, which may be subject to estate taxes.

small business deduction—a special tax deduction provided under the Income Tax Act for active business earned by a Canadian-controlled private corporation.

sole proprietor—an individual who is the sole owner of a business that has not been incorporated.

special needs dependents—individuals that are dependent on family members or the state due to physical or mental infirmity.

spousal trust—an inter vivos or testamentary trust under which the settlor's spouse is entitled to all of the trust income. No person other than the spouse is entitled to capital, as long as the spouse is alive.

springing power of attorney—a power of attorney that takes effect if the donor becomes mentally incapacitated.

statutory duties—duties imposed by provincial law on trustees.

stock options—a contractual right provided by a corporation to allow an investor to acquire shares at a future time at a predetermined price.

stop-loss rules—rules under the Income Tax Act that reduce a capital loss on the disposition of shares in a private corporation by the amount of tax-free capital dividends previously received on those shares.

succession duties—a tax that used to be imposed at both the federal and provincial level on the value of property owned at the time of death (similar to U.S. estate taxes). Succession duties were repealed after the introduction of taxes on capital gains.

sunset provision—legislation that is set to expire at a predetermined date unless extended by new legislation.

systematic withdrawals—a contractual feature of an investment that provides for regular withdrawals or the surrender of units to provide income to the owner.

T

term insurance—insurance where the premium increases at regular intervals and coverage expires at a predetermined age.

testamentary trust—a trust that takes effect upon the death of a property's owner. A trustee administers the trustor property for the beneficiaries specified in the will.

testator—a man who has made a will.

testatrix—a woman who has made a will.

transferor—a property owner who sells or otherwise disposes of a property.

trustee—a person who takes legal title to property and administers it for the benefit of the beneficiaries.

U

universal life insurance—a permanent insurance policy where the insurance and investment components are clearly segregated. Significant flexibility in investing and managing the performance of the policy is offered.

unrealized capital gains—a term that describes the appreciation in value of capital property, prior to the actual sale or disposition of that property.

V

vested contributions—contributions under a Registered Pension Plan that are owned by the plan member, even though the actual payment of benefits may be deferred.

Index